THE
10 LAWS
OF
TRUST
EXPANDED EDITION

JOEL PETERSON

with David A. Kaplan

THE 10 LAWS OF TRUST

EXPANDED EDITION

BUILDING THE BONDS THAT MAKE A BUSINESS GREAT

HarperCollins
LEADERSHIP

An Imprint of HarperCollins

Published by HarperCollins Leadership, an imprint of HarperCollins Focus LLC.

ISBN 978-1-4002-1674-1 (eBook)
ISBN 978-1-4002-1673-4 (HC)

Library of Congress Cataloguing-in-Publication Data

Library of Congress Control Number: 2019936547

Printed in the United States of America

19 20 21 22 LSC 10 9 8 7 6 5 4 3 2 1

To Diana, my trusted partner of forty-six years

"A man who trusts nobody is apt to be
a man nobody trusts."

—HAROLD MACMILLAN

"To be trusted is a greater compliment than
to be loved."

—GEORGE MACDONALD

· CONTENTS ·

CONTENTS

BY STEPHEN COVEY

I'LL NEVER FORGET THE day I met Joel Peterson. It was in November 1985. I had recently been hired by Trammell Crow Company, which at the time was the largest real estate development company in the United States. Joel was serving as its chief financial officer and its de facto strategist.

As a young professional working in my first "real" job, meeting the man who was considered the number-two person in the firm was obviously a big deal to me. Yet, what I remember most to this day was the extraordinary reputation Joel had with seemingly *everyone* in the firm. At a relatively young age, he was already a legend, and everyone talked about not only his brilliance, but also his integrity—and in equal parts. After meeting and spending time with him, I was similarly impressed by both his character and competence, commenting to my wife: "Everybody trusts Joel. He's who I want to be like in business."

It was a great thrill to me years later to have the chance to be personally mentored by Joel when he served as vice chairman of Covey Leadership Center, the firm founded by my father, the late Dr. Stephen R. Covey. I was serving as the company's CEO, and under Joel's guidance I learned many things that significantly influenced my leadership, including the judgment that flows from a broad perspective he called "all things considered," the preeminent importance of focusing on creating value for clients, and the power of simplicity. Through my association with Joel, I also experienced firsthand the impact of credibility and trust. Partly as a result of his influence, I focused intentionally on building a high-trust culture within our organization and with all of our stakeholders. That focus became a game changer for us. Our performance dramatically improved—and we had a lot more fun along the way!

Having since devoted my life and work around what I feel called to do—to help leaders and organizations create and leverage trust—I was humbled and honored when Joel invited me to write the foreword for this superb book *The 10 Laws of Trust*.

Before you begin to read this book, I would like to extend a personal invitation to you. I invite you to consider a particularly challenging business situation or relationship you're currently facing. Assume you have a good grasp of your current circumstances and how you arrived there—but the way forward isn't clear.

Now imagine you will have personal access to unparalleled insight and advice from a business leader, investor, and teacher who has worked firsthand with over 2,300 businesses, hundreds of partners, and thousands of leaders over a forty-year career, and who has also taught thousands of future leaders at Stanford. Further, imagine that this insight and advice will be given to you in a way that is both extremely engaging and highly practical.

That's exactly what's available to you in *The 10 Laws of Trust*. In this remarkable book, you can gain profound insight, wisdom, skill, and courage to move forward in a situation or relationship you're currently facing—as well as in any other challenging situation or, for that matter, any exciting opportunity in life.

Let me share why I can say this so confidently. For over twenty-five years I have been focused on helping people understand and implement the power of trust so that they can access the increased speed, lower cost, higher energy, and fundamental joys that come from trusting and being trusted. In the process, I have learned three fundamental truths about trust.

1 **Trust is an economic driver.** As I analyzed my research and experience to write my own book, *The Speed of Trust*, it became unarguably clear to me that trust is not merely a soft, "nice to have" social virtue; it's also an economic driver, always affecting both the speed at which we can move and the cost of everything involved. Put simply, high trust is a

dividend; low trust is a tax. In fact, in our increasingly low-trust world, trust has literally become the new currency of our global economy. Joel's sharing of personal experiences and his astute observation and analysis of headline business-news events over the past several decades support this reality. The companies, leaders, and educators he cites in this book underscore the fact that lasting success is derived from following enduring principles—particularly trust.

2 **Trust is the one thing that changes everything.** Trust is the number one leadership competency needed today, principally because of how it affects every other competency leaders need to have. All the things we need to do well as leaders—innovating, collaborating, partnering, teaming, attracting and retaining people, engaging people, executing, selling, leading change—we can do better if we start with trust. Trust is a *multiplier* for all these competencies, eventually creating a ripple effect that can positively impact not only our organizations but ultimately, all of society.

3 **Trust is a learnable competency.** Trust is not just the domain of a privileged few with charisma or certain personality characteristics. Trust is a competency, a set of attitudes and skills that can be acquired and sustained by anyone who's willing to pay the price. As Joel's work illustrates, enduring organizations are created by leaders and people who excel in this competency—who understand and practice the

fundamental beliefs of *being credible* and *behaving* in ways that inspire trust. Joel gives us a wonderfully comprehensive blueprint of how to do it with his 10 Laws.

Joel's book is powerfully aligned with these three truths. In addition, as I've already mentioned, he himself is an amazingly credible source. He's built, led, invested in, and guided highly successful organizations. He's built high-trust cultures. He has lived and modeled these 10 Laws he espouses. Each of the three elements in his definition of trust—character, competence and authority—I have personally seen him demonstrate with excellence. I've witnessed his deep integrity, his competence as an organizational leader and investor, and the principled way he exercises and aligns authority.

Because Joel presents the 10 Laws in a way that is immensely practical, they are relatively simple to apply (though not easy). When I began my study of trust, I found that many of the books published on the topic were either too simplistic and naïve or too philosophical and academic. They shared theories, but not enough practices to enable people to successfully incorporate them in their work and lives. Unlike those books, Joel's 10 Laws simultaneously blend enduring principles with powerful practical applications you can implement immediately in the real world.

To me, one of the most impactful parts of Joel's book is his final chapter on restoring trust. This is a subject I also explored in *The Speed of Trust*, and I am convinced this is an essential focus in today's society with so many broken leaders, broken promises, and broken cultures that all need to be made whole again through commitment and alignment with enduring principles. My father wisely taught, "You can't talk your way out of a problem you behaved your way into." While I agree, I've also learned that you can often *behave* your way out of a problem you behaved your way into. Indeed, in many situations, you *can* restore trust, and Joel's experience and insight demonstrate where it might be possible, where it might be wise, and how it might be done. What incredible hope this gives to those who have been struggling with issues around broken trust!

For all of these reasons—and more—I am firmly convinced that the time you spend considering your current business challenge as you read *The 10 Laws of Trust* will pay off handsomely for you. But further, it will give you a solid foundation for resolving other issues in the future, and—even more important—for creating behaviors and cultures of trust that will enable you from the outset to avoid many of the challenges that derail other companies and leaders, and instead be positioned to maximize all that can go right.

Bottom line: In our uncertain, ever-changing world, Joel has given us a powerful and practical foundation of unchanging principles. As we understand and apply the 10 Laws, we will become people and leaders who can be trusted—and who trust others. It's my belief and hope that Joel's book will help us develop the perspective and judgment to inspire and extend trust deliberately so that each of us can enjoy greater prosperity, energy, and joy in all dimensions of our lives. As we do this, the ultimate end will be that together we will be able to increase trust—and the benefits of trust—throughout the world. And that's how we will continue to make the world a better place for us all.

Stephen M. R. Covey
Author of *The New York Times* and #1 *Wall Street Journal* bestselling book
The Speed of Trust, and cofounder of FranklinCovey's Trust Practice

THE 10 LAWS OF TRUST

EXPANDED EDITION

I LACK THE PARANOIA GENE. Despite the prescriptions in any number of manuals on management advice dating to Machiavelli, I'm naturally inclined to trust other people: I expect others to be trustworthy, and I'm predisposed to trust that people will do what they say they'll do.

My life is a testament to the power of trust—as board chairman, teacher, real estate entrepreneur, growth-capital investor, father of seven, and spouse of forty-six years. My parents trusted me; my wife believed I'd figure things out long before I actually did; my early partners granted me independence based on little more than instinct. These high-trust relationships changed my life and allowed me to achieve far more than my natural abilities would have predicted. And I've accomplished much more by trusting others than I'd ever have achieved through wariness.

Indeed, I've learned that to trust means taking a leap of faith—a necessary part of giving over control to another. Through sad experience, I'm now better at selecting whom to trust and at insisting on establishing a culture in which trust can flourish. I've come to appreciate that it's a dynamic process, with rules that must be maintained, with results that must be authenticated, and with breaches that may need repair. But I'm no Pollyanna: I recognize that one cannot eliminate the possibility of peril. Trust inescapably contemplates risk.

So why trust? Because it works, most of the time. Not only do people accomplish more in a collaborative spirit when seeking win-win outcomes than when setting up the paraphernalia of paranoia, but they're simply much happier when dealing in a world of harmony and cooperation.

When it comes to building great companies, a leader's job isn't to make it to the top of the mountain alone. Instead, the task is to help others reach peaks *they* want to climb but might not be able to without the help of a leader. I've found that reaching for the highest summits typically leaves little time for mistrust—or exhaustive reliance on compliance manuals. Entrepreneurs may be criticized for having insufficient controls in place or trusting partners too readily. Maybe so in some instances. But the cost of the alternative can be much higher: Ever-present suspicion, double-riveted legal agreements, caution and caginess in interpersonal dealings—the touchstones of mistrust—can slow things down, drive away the most trustworthy people, and inhibit innovation. High-trust ventures, on the other hand, require team members like climbers attempting a technical ascent to be belayed, dependent on each other to reach the summit together. Experiencing that kind of trust is truly exhilarating.

The goals of this book are to (1) examine what trust is, (2) present methods for harnessing it, and (3) consider how to restore trust or recover from its breach. After half a century of living a life devoted to leadership, I hope the 10 Laws of Trust that follow will help readers build organizations with higher trust, as well as become happier, more optimistic, and more successful themselves.

WHEN TALKING WITH READERS after writing the first edition of this book, I discovered two things. First, most leaders remain blissfully ignorant of their team's existing levels of (mis)trust. Second, few team members are strangers to betrayal; they have valid reasons for their mistrust. Within today's remarkably polarized society, many have learned to mistrust news outlets, political leaders, and society's most fundamental institutions (courts, banks, churches, and schools).

The thesis of *The 10 Laws of Trust* is that leaders can consciously build a high-trust culture, and that a culture of high trust represents a powerful competitive advantage. But engineering high-trust cultures rests on knowing baseline trust levels of team members. And because virtually all will have experienced betrayal in some form at some time in their lives, it is, likewise, vital to know how to overcome the derivative wariness.

The new material in this expanded edition is aimed at (1) assessing existing organizational trust levels, and (2) removing the stubborn residue of betrayal. Thus, I've added two items as appendices to this second edition:

1 **A Diagnostic.** This is a simple 10-question assessment tool to give leaders a measure of existing trust levels. Having helped thousands of leaders increase trust within— and across—teams, FranklinCovey has developed this survey as a starting point for assessing the degree of difficulty presented by the road to high trust.

2 **Real-Life Cases of Betrayal.** To my own personal experience with mutual betrayal, I've added two disguised business-school cases with questions that provide material for teams to discuss how to build or restore trust:

- **Case 1:** A bank's violation of a customer's trust.
- **Case 2:** A lawyer's betrayal of a friend and client.

These tales of suspicion, power, and greed might make one despair unless, without knowing how to survive them, one grows from them and avoids repeating them.

This new material aims to provoke discussion that will empower readers to avoid betrayal and recover from it in their own organization and in the lives of team members. Other than my own story, the cases have been disguised. While the case facts are accurate, all names, locations, and other references are fictional.

At a minimum, these tales of betrayal remind us that to trust necessarily means to take risks. But to *decide not to trust* is to take the greater risk that virtually ensures an unfulfilling life—to say nothing of depriving oneself of benefits that flow naturally from well-grounded, high-trust relationships.

Because betrayal is the occasional offspring of trust, repairing (or surviving) betrayal is vital to regaining the confidence to once again offer one's trust, whether confronting betrayal in the moment, overcoming its toxic effects when discovered after the fact, or reconciling oneself to permanent loss and alienation.

Not all trust winds up in betrayal. Indeed, just the opposite is true: trust usually offers large and immediate dividends, both economic and emotional. But any discussion of trust must recognize that betrayal can happen. The new material in this expanded edition is especially for readers who've experienced betrayal—or who fear it so much, they resist taking trust's requisite leap of faith.

THE POWER OF TRUST

IN BUSINESS, AS IN life, trust is elemental. We all cherish it. Most of us think we deserve it. Few of us think we violate it. But what exactly is it? At its core, trust means willingly ceding a measure of control to another—be it a person, an organization, or an institution—and without the apparent safety nets of a binding contract or other means of coercion in place. Although we trust with an expectation others will respond in kind, vulnerability is the psychological hallmark of trust. We're taking a risk, sometimes based on limited evidence. Trust is a leap of faith rooted in optimism.

We take trust for granted, not conscious of how it pervades relationships. Partners rely on partners; employers on employees; companies on each other; nations on other nations; families on other family members. And in a world in which the peer-to-peer economy is gaining ascendance—with individuals sharing cars, boats, and apartments—trust is all the more indispensable. Understanding the underpinnings of trust, therefore, is increasingly important as companies become more global, more competitive, and more diverse culturally and demographically. Each new thread of well-founded trust adds strength and richness to the complex tapestry of our interwoven economic and personal lives.

But trust doesn't just happen. It takes initiation, nurture, evaluation, and repair. Trust is earned. Trust builds over time, fostered not only by decency but also by enlightened self-interest, a recognition that trust works to everyone's benefit. As a lubricant, trust accelerates decision making, results in agreements that are both durable and flexible, and makes life infinitely more pleasant. Trust creates a bond among an organization's associates, customers, and suppliers, which in turn accelerates its ability to deliver on its promises to each group. But trust is neither an end unto itself nor merely a technique for achieving a desired outcome. Trust is the operating system for a life well lived.

There is power in being trustworthy. In the economy of trust, what goes around comes around. The more we look out for others, the more they look out for us. The more we trust, the more we are trusted. When trust is the medium of exchange, people collaborate and altruism can grow again to everyone's benefit.

Evolutionary biologists David Sloan Wilson and E. O. Wilson propose a thought experiment for the relative power of selfishness versus generosity: Two groups are placed on separate islands with no way to communicate. On one island, it's each person for himself. On the other, everybody works together to achieve broader goals. A few generations later you'll find two very different societies: one in a state of constant, near-psychopathic conflict, the other successful and harmonious. Summarizing the essential argument for building trust, these scientists conclude: "Selfishness beats altruism within groups. Altruistic groups beat selfish groups. Everything else is commentary."[1]

Put simply, high-trust (altruistic) organizations prevail over low-trust (selfish) organizations, and over time, high-trust leaders are more successful than low-trust leaders. Contrast the high trust levels of the legendary teams built by Alan Mulally at Boeing and then at Ford, with those at Enron, where temporary success ended in spectacular failure. Just as important, selfish (low-trust) groups, besides losing to altruistic (high-trust) groups, suffer misery within their ranks. One need only review Stanford University professor Bob Sutton's bestseller *The No Asshole Rule* to see how untrusting workplace behaviors wound productivity and morale.

Like air, trust is invisible, and when abundant, it is taken for granted. But again like air, when trust is in short supply, people must find ways to cope. When suspicions arise, people reach for legal documents, policy manuals, and other preemptive measures—the scar tissue of strained trust. Worse, when trust breaks down altogether, responses to the ensuing wreckage can vary from giving up altogether to grabbing power—from threatening to litigating.

Make no mistake: Building and maintaining trust is hard work. Trust can be fragile. One bad actor can damage it. A single act of deceit can destroy a reputation for being trustworthy that was built over a lifetime. Be it in the boardroom or in statecraft or in literature—Hewlett-Packard or Julius Caesar or Othello—betrayal is poison. Bernie Madoff's investment firm and Bernie Ebbers's WorldCom will forever live in the annals of capitalist infamy. There's a good reason why being called an Iago is among the worst stains on a reputation.

But if you live in a world of suspicion or selfishness, you may not even be aware that you and your necessarily low-trust teammates are like runners on a relay team lugging around heavy oxygen tanks in order to cope with the short supply of trust. You may not notice that your attention has shifted from the potential of posting a winning time to avoiding the risk of finishing last. Your energy is spent securing a replacement for the air you'd enjoy naturally in a high-trust environment. You look past innovation, optimization, and mutual gain in order to obsess over threats, downsides, and coercion. You look out only for yourself. As a result, low trust begets even lower trust.

The following 10 Laws of Trust lay out attitudes and behaviors you can count on to increase the odds that the flow of trust in your enterprise will not be interrupted. Their implementation will arrest the decline of trust and keep you from burning all of your energy to protect against low-trust behavior on the part of others.

Scientists point out that a good theory is one that predicts outcomes, giving us a sense of causality. One should expect a correlation between certain behaviors and the development of predictable trust within a team. And while no one has scientifically tested these 10 Laws, I've spent a lifetime assessing them to figure out what works and what doesn't. My bottom line is that investing in trust works to create abundance and is far superior to hoarding power, harboring suspicions, or barricading oneself behind gotcha controls.

Being smart about whom to trust, when to trust, and how to nurture organizational trust is key to implementing the 10 Laws. Understanding the following truths about the very nature of trust—its preconditions, varieties, underpinnings, and risks—prepares a leader to undertake the job of building a high-trust organization.

1 **Trust—well-grounded—depends on three conditions.** To safely and reliably allow others to act on our behalf—which is what we mean by trusting them—we must be able to count on three underpinnings: character, competence, and authority.

- **Character** means that those we trust will value our interests as their own.
- **Competence** means that those we trust have the requisite intelligence, ability, and training to achieve our best interests.

- **Authority** means that those we trust are empowered
  to deliver on promises.

When all three conditions are present, trust develops naturally, almost reflexively. But when any of the three is absent,
trust must take a holiday. To trust in the absence of any of
these three elements is not smart but naïve—and eventual betrayal is almost certain.

Those who meet these three conditions for being granted
our trust (character + competence + authority) almost always
possess a broader view of life's purpose than merely securing
the best personal outcome in every single transaction, in every
conversation, in every negotiation. People who see life as a
marathon rather than a sprint, as a narrative in which everything eventually connects, are the best bets for long-term trust.
These individuals tend to have an enlightened, all-things-con-
sidered self-interest. They choose to act with the belief that
trustworthy behavior pays dividends, if only in the harmony
that comes from a lifetime of durable, high-trust relationships.
Possessing a bone-deep belief that they are accountable to
more than just their own interests, they are simply unlikely to
betray another's trust.

2 **There are three types of trust.** In building a high-
trust organization, one must understand the three forms
that trust can take: reciprocal, representative, and pseudo trust:

Reciprocal (or mutual) trust exists when people advance each other's interests out of love, duty, or enlightened self-interest. Most prevalent between spouses and other family members, mutual trust can also be found between interdependent business partners. As with a relay team, the practitioners (and beneficiaries) of reciprocal trust can be confident their combined performance will exceed the best efforts of any single member. Thus, in reciprocal-trust relationships, the results of individual efforts are multiplied and outcomes are predictably superior to any one member's independent efforts. Shared goals are achieved faster and more durably than when everyone is on their own—mistrustful of colleagues, wary of leaders. Nobody on a relay team worries that the next person to get the baton is going to run a faster lap. And no single runner will beat a 4x100 relay team.

Representative trust is the more common form of reliance on others. When electing officials or, say, hiring a lawyer, we hand over our trust, expecting it to be honored in return. Young children rely on parents to represent them, and parents honor children's trust by protecting their interests. Similarly, doctors and other professionals honor our trust by safeguarding our welfare, asking that we provide good information in exchange. The uneven economy of representative stewardship makes possible the specialization needed to achieve complex goals. Absent reliable representative trust, society breaks down. Nobody can produce, or be an expert at, everything; we all must trust professionals to represent our interests faithfully.

Finally, under the label of trust operates its counterfeit—**pseudo trust**—the temporary alignment of one's self-interests with those of another. While pseudo trust necessarily forms the basis for many contractual economic relationships, this convenient arrangement shouldn't be mistaken for the real thing. As a governor of short-term actions, it has less to offer and may actually undermine efforts to build a high-trust culture of collaboration. In the end, pseudo trust will almost invariably lead to short-term, episodic thinking and, when conditions change, eventual betrayal.

Indeed, many who have not paid the price to build genuine trust temporarily accrue some of trust's benefits by simply aligning with the self-interested. Pseudo trust is dangerous, however. Hitching one's interests to a counterparty can feel like authentic trust, but only until respective interests diverge. Like mafia dons thriving by mutual dependence on fear and greed, individuals in a pseudo-trust arrangement (for example, the enemy of my enemy is my friend) often discover that it rarely leads to more than the fleeting security of common interests. Useful for a season, it is destined to fail as circumstances change. Voters often trust politicians to back causes that matter to them without realizing that a politician's primary interest is being reelected. These voters are destined to experience the betrayal of a flip-flop—a breach of pseudo trust—the minute their cause no longer appeals to a majority of a politician's constituents.

3 **Underlying motivators establish potential trust levels.** Intuitively, we know that different levels of trust exist in different kinds of organizations. No-trust organizations, such as prisons, rely on force. Low-trust organizations, such as dictatorships, live on fear. The motivator in most business organizations is reward. Only high-trust organizations are motivated by duty and love, by a sense of meaning and mission—even a calling. The bonds between parent and child often yield this sort of trust within a family, for example.

While combinations of these motivators are present at different times in most organizations, only those organizations in which exists a sense of responsibility to all constituents, and a sense of meaning or mission, will consistently be moved by higher-level motivators such as duty or love. As Figure 1 illustrates, there is a hierarchy of motivators. The half-life of the motivating force increases as one moves from left (force) to right (love), and as the source of the motivator moves from extrinsic to intrinsic.

Naturally, trust grows when people relate to the mission of an organization and have leaders and employees committed to that mission. What tends to motivate people within any organization tells you what level of trust you might realistically hope for.

TRUST LEVEL BY ORGANIZATION

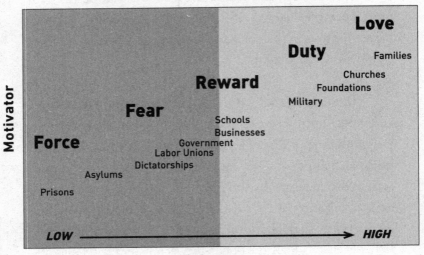

FIGURE 1. Trust Level by Organization

The good news for leaders is that other than in prisons and asylums, trust levels are not fixed by the nature of the organization. As a leader, you can move the needle. The goal of any leader should be to move to the high-trust end of the spectrum and thereby to reliance on mission, caring, meaning, and duty. Here's where adhering to the 10 Laws of Trust can make all the difference.

4 **As trust declines, people grab power.** Another way to contrast low-trust organizations with high-trust organizations is to compare the role of power in achieving desired

POWER	Low Trust	High Trust
NATURE	**A personal asset** *(owed to self)*	**A stewardship** *(owed to interests of those granting power)*
SOURCE	**Politics** ✓ Breaking Rules ✓ Making Credible Threats ✓ Self-Promotion ✓ Employing Series of Techniques	**Trust** ✓ Knowledge ✓ Competence ✓ Judgment ✓ Hard Work ✓ Fiduciary Behavior
PURPOSE	**To get stuff** *(money, health, intrinsic need)* *...and the tautological "getting things done"*	**To achieve common goals** *(consistent with values)*
MINDSET	"It's all about **ME**."	"It's all about the **mission**."
WHY?	**Because the world is unjust –** *> I must look out for #1.*	**Because the world is (sometimes) unjust –** *> I must care for those who've empowered me.*

FIGURE 2. How Leaders View Power

ends. In low-trust organizations, power plays the key role in attaining goals. In high-trust organizations, authority is still vital, but it tends to be distributed and is aimed at a shared mission. And it is seen not as a personal asset to be wielded by leaders for their own benefit but as both a duty owed to those granting it and a responsibility to those over whom it extends. Figure 2 compares how leaders view power in low- and high-trust organizations.

Stanford professor Jeff Pfeffer asserts in *Power: Why Some People Have It—and Others Don't* that power flows to those who break rules, make credible threats, self-promote, and use its exercise as a technique to coerce others—the essence of a low-trust organization.[2] In high-trust organizations, however, such behaviors are anathema. Pfeffer's thesis ignores the essence of high-trust organizations and their leaders. Power in high-trust organizations derives not from scheming or techniques. It is less imposed than freely granted. Durable power derives from trust and is distributed as an expression of trust.

As Rod Kramer, another Stanford professor, has remarked, "Power without trust seems like a hollow victory for a leader and a thin platform from which to lead." Ultimately, for all the bare-knuckled, power-grasping tyrants who have succeeded (if only for a season), there are many other leaders who have labored to create the greatest good for the greatest number of people. These high-trust leaders have developed durable organizations and flexible, trusting teams working together to achieve more than any of them would have accomplished individually.

5 **Trust risks betrayal.** Although trust relationships can, of course, terminate by mutual agreement, they occasionally end in betrayal. In fact, betrayal requires the existence of trust in the first place. Indeed, all three forms of trust are subject to potential betrayal: pseudo trust by its very nature, and reciprocal and representative trust to the extent you've trusted someone without character, competence, and authority.

Betrayal can demolish the trust earned over a lifetime, probably never to be rebuilt. So people naturally worry about balancing the need to trust with the recognition that treachery may lurk. If betrayal lies ever in wait, what then is one to do? Can one ever rely on a handshake, trust someone's word, take it on faith? Must trust be carefully evaluated to be certain it is well-grounded before taking the leap? In short, how do you know if you're dealing with George "I Cannot Tell a Lie" Washington or Benedict Arnold?

The potential for betrayal can be minimized by

- Making sure all the elements of trust (character, competence, and authority) are well established
- Understanding the three forms trust takes (reciprocal, representative, and pseudo) and recognizing that the betrayal of pseudo trust may only be a matter of time
- Building a culture rooted in the 10 Laws of Trust

To be sure, trust risks occasional betrayal. But the absence of trust *is* betrayal—of everyone condemned to work for coercive leaders. Because "[a]ltruistic groups beat selfish groups," organizations deprived of trust are destined to be surpassed by those animated by trust.

IN SUMMARY, THE ODDS of building high-trust organizations through consistent application of the 10 Laws of Trust increase when their leaders first gain a solid understanding of the nature of trust, as outlined above and restated here:

- Well-grounded trust depends on accurately assessing the character, competence, and authority of those to whom we consider granting our trust.

- Of the three common strains of trust (reciprocal, representative, and pseudo), pseudo trust is the least reliable, as it is stable only when interests are aligned.
- Different organizations have inherently different potential for trust depending on the primary motivators used by those in charge (force, fear, reward, duty, or love).
- When trust is low or absent, the vacuum will be filled by those who depend on power to drive outcomes.
- The risk of betrayal can be diminished by hiring and promoting those willing to adhere to the 10 Laws.

Over time, high-trust enterprises will successfully compete with their benighted counterparts obsessed with politics, self-protection, and self-aggrandizing power. The satisfaction that derives from collaboration, the innovation that flows from interdependent teams, the joy that springs from knowing you can trust those with whom you work—all are well worth the effort required to understand the nature of trust and to internalize and live by its laws.

START WITH PERSONAL
INTEGRITY

THE WATCHWORD OF ANY high-trust organization is *in-tegrity*—and it has to start with those at the top. Leaders in high-trust organizations must serve as archetypes of integrity, and not just at the office or during business hours. For an organization to develop durable trust among all team members, its leaders must be consistent and predictable, having integrated (1) private with public scruples, (2) competence with benevolence, and (3) action with utterance.

Building a high-trust organization, rather than relying on a vague, generalized sense of honor, requires working to establish integrity as its foundation. Without leaders who have integrity in the first place, a leader's efforts will be perceived as hollow techniques aimed at fooling people into ceding power.

Some leaders try to compartmentalize their lives into private and public arenas, filing violations of personal trust under the "private" label. But no matter their competence or charisma, leaders who violate commitments to family, friends, or associates are unlikely to build enduring organizational trust. Personal corruption cannot comfortably coexist with long-term public trust. Even those in the nether regions of an organization will eventually figure out whether their leaders act in a manner consistent with their words and with the stated values of the organization.

The gap between what a leader says and does is at the heart of trust. For an example, one need look no further than the highly publicized breach of trust involving David Petraeus. Over the course of four decades, he became a decorated four-star general in the US Army, in command of all coalition forces in Iraq. Next, he was director of the CIA—confirmed unanimously by the Senate—and was even mentioned as a potential presidential candidate. And then it was over. In 2012, barely a year into his CIA tenure, he resigned under pressure, citing an extramarital affair and his mishandling of classified information.

Petraeus's downfall occurred because of the disconnect between how he behaved privately and who he said he was publicly. His story is a particularly sad instance of the loss of legacy because of a private violation of trust. It proves how fragile—but vital—the connection is. Because Petraeus gave so many years of capable service, he comes as close as anyone to being an exception to the First Law of Trust: being trusted in one arena while violating trust in another. But even one so esteemed professionally could not maintain his leadership once the discontinuity between private and public integrity became apparent. As ABC News anchor Diane Sawyer noted, "People will forgive you for not being the leader you want to be—but never for not being the leader you claim to be."

Meeting the high-integrity test does not depend only on perceived benevolence. Because one can have a good heart and still be utterly disorganized, unpredictable, or unreliable, the second element of integrity is even more central to trust. This is the requirement that we complement our benevolence with competence. We've all known people with high character who can't seem to figure out how to be on time, complete assignments when due, or to carry out simple tasks such as double checking what doesn't matter to them personally. While we might trust them to sign checks for us because they would never think of being dishonest, we can't trust them to be our CFOs or lawyers.

Growing up as the child of a homemaker and a research scientist, I absorbed lessons in both of these elements of integrity from my parents. My mother was as kindhearted as anyone I've known, passing the benevolence test with flying colors, never doing anything to deceive anyone. My father, though not as reliably kind, was deeply competent and capable of delivering results. Neither had mastered the other's chief reason to be trusted. I could count on my mother's heart, but not always her ability to deliver. I could count on my father's reliability, but not always on his benevolence. Each had an incomplete version of the integrity required to build a high-trust enterprise.

In many organizations, integrity is emphasized without sufficient focus on both notions. But building enduring trust within an organization requires not only integrating private honor with public honor and benevolence with competence—it also requires removing the gaps between what we say and what we do.

In other words, organizations will not, and should not, trust leaders if they're merely virtuous. Followers also need to count on leaders for competent execution, and for little space between action and utterance. In the business world, for example, Starbucks employees tend to trust their place of employment not only because they feel it's a virtuous company but also because they believe that its CEO, Howard Schultz, does what he says he'll do, be it about things like the primacy of health insurance or the company's commitment to hiring veterans.

All trust begins with character. And because character embodies both forms of integrity, what follows are ways to think about personal integrity as an underpinning of trust. Although these observations may seem intuitive, you might be surprised to learn that some leaders view them as trivial, having little to do with *realpolitik* in the boardroom, in the workplace, or during negotiations. The politics of power, rather than integrity is, in their view, the coin of the corporate realm.

While no one can claim perfect congruence between private and public actions, or complete reliability and predictability around results, there's a continuum along which we all operate. The further we get from any of these dimensions of integrity, the more likely we are to rely on carrots and sticks and other more primitive applications of power to achieve objectives. And the closer we get to integrity in all of its dimensions, the more likely our organizations will enjoy the benefits of self-directed employees, innovation, and lower turnover.

In seeking the kind of integrity on which leaders can build organizational trust, they should always remember to:

1 **Sync words with actions.** Individuals who run things must demonstrate the way they want business to be done as well as the way they want others to be treated. Talking alone won't cut it. Leaders must embody the spirit they want the team to adopt. Just as people pick up on phoniness and instinctively spot say-do gaps, they recognize—and trust—authenticity. Just as kids see parents as examples, for good or bad, team members watch leaders for cues.

Incongruence spreads—first to other individuals, then to pockets within a company, and finally to the organization as a whole. So when leaders miss an opportunity to exemplify core values, they sow distrust. Whatever else observers criticized in Steve Jobs's management style, nobody doubted his commitment to design, even at the risk of market share. Other foibles earned him a reputation as an imperious boss, but many eventually came to trust him, in part because he predictably spent time, money, and energy on exactly what he claimed were his values.

George Steinbrenner, the late owner of the New York Yankees, preached the values of philanthropy and kindness. He, too, could be a management bully. But when Steinbrenner died in 2010 at age eighty, scores of people came forward to tell of his private acts of generosity: unpublicized scholarships for poor children, quiet donations to the families of fallen police officers, letters and visits to past employees and strangers in need of support. Those kinds of quiet actions—backing up his words—carry continuing power for the Yankee and Steinbrenner brands. While generosity does not equal the kind of integrity required by the First Law of Trust, Steinbrenner showed a certain measure of consistency between values and actions upon which trust could build.

2 **Avoid hypocrisy.** A leader can't build trust on skills, charisma, and expertise alone. Trustworthy leaders show respect, consider the welfare of others, and keep their word. This doesn't end at the close of the workday; leaders who can't manage commitments outside the office are far less likely to establish enduring trust with colleagues, suppliers, or customers. If they pretend to have virtues or competencies they don't possess, leaders risk creating cynicism and a loss of trust. Better to promise less and deliver more in order to build trust.

3 **Work on establishing integrity as a habit.** Leaders who strive to do the right thing under any circumstance have developed the discipline to consider the long run, to

subordinate themselves to the mission of the enterprise, and to act as a fiduciary for others. Trustworthy leaders are intentional about "fixing things" in themselves, about receiving feedback, and about making changes based on that feedback. Just as a great mechanic keeps a race car in top condition, high-trust individuals monitor and tune their behavior, striving to do better.

In my own case, I decided early on to turn my values into reality before the temptation to violate them appeared. I wrote out a plan to reserve time with family. Shortly after I joined Trammell Crow Company, the founder called me at home on a Sunday, asking me to come to the office to discuss a deal. Although flattered, I nervously informed him that I had reserved Sundays for family and would see him as early as he wanted on Monday morning. This boundary established to me, and to my boss, the values I intended to keep.

ANYONE WANTING TO BUILD a high-trust organization must start by looking in the mirror. Doing so will inevitably reveal shortcomings—breaches of integrity—where our actions don't reflect our words, or our private behavior isn't up to our public image. Even if you're not where you want to be, team members who see leaders working on shortcomings will tend to trust them, and enterprise-wide trust will grow.

. . .

KEY QUESTION

LAW 1: INTEGRITY. Leaders in my organization *consistently* align their behaviors with the principles to which they aspire.

1.	2.	3.	4.	5.
Strongly Disagree	Generally Disagree	Neutral	Generally Agree	Strongly Agree

---

INVEST IN RESPECT

Personal integrity means doing what you say you're going to do, and that your actions will consistently reflect your principles—publicly and privately. While personal integrity is the foundation for a culture of organizational trust, leaders must also be looking to spread trust across an organization. How? By practicing the art of respect—for everybody, in ways large and small.

Respect is the currency of trust, the way it's exchanged among people. Like any attitude or behavior, respect requires focus, awareness, and practice. The trust that grows out of respect depends more on the value placed on individuals than on management techniques or policy statements. And it is reflected in simple, daily interactions.

Nothing shows greater respect for others than to listen to them without an agenda. That means listening not to agree or disagree (or to stall as you prepare a response), but simply to understand. The late author and thought leader Stephen R. Covey, one of the most effective leaders I've worked with, suggested you should always try to "capture" another person's point of view, especially in a potential disagreement. Covey would begin, "If I understand what you're saying," then describe the opposing viewpoint to that person's satisfaction. Powerfully demonstrating respect, he could often state the other's position better than the other person had. From this model, I've learned to ask people, "What alternatives did you consider when coming up with your recommendation?" Listening carefully, I've learned to withhold judgment until I've understood how they thought about a problem, not just how they decided to solve it. Many have told me that this is a sign of respect, and one that forces them to prepare carefully.

Leaders further demonstrate and encourage respect when they empower team members, celebrate their contributions, and help them learn from missteps. In his book *Social Physics: How Good Ideas Spread*, Professor Alex "Sandy" Pentland of the Massachusetts Institute of Technology, a computer scientist who directs the school's Human Dynamics Laboratory, wrote:

> It is not simply the brightest who have the best ideas; it is those who are best at harvesting them from others. It is not only the most determined who drive change; it is those who most fully engage with like-minded people.

And it is not wealth or prestige that best motivates people; it is respect and help from peers.[1]

Showing respect in an organization doesn't center only on those in the executive suite. You'll know you've got a high-trust organization when you find leaders showing respect to people at every level, especially those from whom they stand to gain the least. Watch chairman and CEO Marc Benioff walk around the vast offices of Salesforce and you'll see he's engaged with his people. He knows details—not just about board members and major shareholders, but also about receptionists and drivers in different cities.

Trusted leaders show respect by seeking feedback from individuals outside their inner circles. They remember names of colleagues and even the names of their colleagues' children and friends—not to score points, but because they care. Sincerity matters. There are many traditional ways to show respect to colleagues, such as recalling birthdays or anniversaries. But here's another thought: Make the boilerplate "How are you doing?" mean something. Most recipients of that throwaway question have been trained to believe you don't really care how they're doing. So try to develop such follow-up responses as "I've noticed you've been away/under pressure/quieter than usual." Likewise, instead of asking, "Is there anything I can do?"—which will seldom elicit a request for help—query, "Could I take something off your plate?" or "Would taking a day off help?"

At Google headquarters, leaders foster interaction up and down the ranks, a form of encouraging cross-team respect. In its various on-campus cafeterias, though the food may be gourmet, the tables are decidedly high school: long and narrow, with too little space behind the chairs. It's intentional. That way, you'll be forced to bump into somebody when you sit down or get up—and thereby interact with a colleague, perhaps a new one. Consultants call such workplace design serendipitous interaction; at Google, employees call it "the Google Bump."

At Hewlett-Packard (HP), back in the day, management let engineers take equipment home to tinker with; they didn't need to ask permission or fill out forms in triplicate. Management showed respect by trusting them to return the equipment, which in turn cemented a stronger bond of trust at HP. This is an example of what Stanford professor Rod Kramer calls "measured trust"—small and imaginative acts that foster reciprocity. Kramer has noted how such policies send a strong signal of trust at little risk.

Just as you can't fake character or integrity, you can't feign respect. Too many leaders—be they a state senator, a neighborhood shopkeeper, or a bank manager—trip up by simply failing to be respectful.

A textbook example of what respect doesn't look like happened at HP in 2007, when the company acknowledged it had spied on its own board in an attempt to discover which directors were leaking information to the press. Private detectives, with apparent knowledge of company officials, impersonated directors and journalists in calls to phone companies to gain access to phone records. This utterly trust-killing activity introduced a sinister cloak-and-dagger term into the lexicon of the digital age: pretexting. More fittingly, it might just have been called lying. Once an icon of Silicon Valley rectitude—the "HP Way" had been thought of as a manual on running a business—the company was ridiculed for a clumsy, disrespectful breach of trust. Even today, in part because of this violation of respect, many see HP as a weakened brand with a bruised reputation.

Respect must also exist beyond an organization's boundaries. It manifests itself (or doesn't) in dealings with suppliers, competitors, and even critics. Indeed, the absence of respect in these contexts may be the most telling; if interactions outside the office reflect genuine interest, employees inside may come to trust that they will not be considered trivial.

Here are four ideas for creating an atmosphere of respect, in which trust can thrive:

1 **Respect is a high-yield investment.** Nothing yields greater dividends in team coherence, employee satisfaction, and organizational momentum than advancing the best interests of the people you work with. Leaders know that as an organization's reputation for respecting everyone becomes ingrained, so do trust levels. More trust means less politics and fewer personal agendas. And without those drags on trust,

people are more productive, more satisfied, and more likely to come up with new ideas.

Many years ago, my Trammell Crow partners recognized that I had long been putting in too many hours on the road. So they bought a weeklong resort vacation for my wife and me. Knowing I'd never accept their condition that I not contact the office for an entire week—or even accept the all-expense-paid vacation—they made all the arrangements with my assistant, bought the tickets, and canceled my appointments. While I wasn't sure about accepting their expression of thanks at the time, I've since thought back on their kindness as a highly meaningful expression of respect. Their investment paid off, as I came back more committed than ever.

2 **Positive always beats negative.** Honoring those who aren't present is an ideal way to show respect for those who are. Steer clear of trash-talking even the competition. If leaders engage in people-bashing, even those who happen to be spared the attack will have legitimate reason to mistrust. Your culture will be better served by celebrating what your own team is doing than by tearing down foes.

Equally important to remember is that even the most distressing situations, such as firing people, can be done in a respectful way, reflecting a process of helping those who will do better elsewhere to get on with things in a dignified manner.

3 **Showing respect isn't the same as being nice.**
Showing respect means more than being deferential.
Indeed, disagreement is often key to great decision making.
Out of respectful debate and dissent can grow the best strategy
and product, as long as everyone agrees after a decision has
been made that they're all rowing together. Nobody thought of
Steve Jobs as nice, yet most of his colleagues most of the time
recognized that he respected good ideas and the people who
advanced them.

Don't confuse being a pleaser with showing respect. Being
genial, pleasant, and helpful can contribute to respectful interactions. But real respect is demonstrated by empowering others,
giving them feedback, making time for their concerns, and expecting them to give their best. People will quickly figure out if
your show of respect is superficial. When I first started teaching at Stanford, Associate Dean Mark Wolfson asked for my
analysis of a faculty housing matter. I worked over the weekend
to research the issues and prepare a memo. I considered this a
profound expression of respect from this highly accomplished
scholar.

4 **Tolerating disrespect allows it to spread.** Just as respect can be catching, disrespect can become a conta-
gion. Every baseball manager knows that out of disrespect in
the dugout grows team conflict that corrodes the quality of
play on the field. The Boston Red Sox of 2011 were infamous
for pitchers who partied in the clubhouse while the rest of the

team was playing. The revelers drank beer and played video games as the team collapsed in the last month of the season. Tolerating such practices can result in the loss of key team members and organizational stability, leaving a business limping for years. Vigilant leaders always look to nip disrespectful practices in the bud. That means no tolerance for backbiting, letting problems fester, or failing to give individuals the feedback they need to improve.

Worse than tolerating disrespect is when leaders initiate disrespectful attitudes about race, gender, age, or ethnicity. But most insidious are the expressions of disrespect that come from failing to post jobs, to interview internal candidates, or to give people warnings and training.

A VIBRANT ATMOSPHERE OF trust is one in which colleagues are constantly showing respect to, and earning respect from, one another. Respect starts with the example set by an organization's leaders. In a trust-driven culture, respect is prized at every level. If building a culture of respect sounds difficult to achieve, that's because it is. But it is a long-term commitment that will pay off, strengthening bonds among teammates and among all with whom they do business.

• • •

KEY QUESTION

LAW 2: RESPECT. Individuals in my organization behave respectfully *to a much greater extent* than they behave disrespectfully in their dealings with each other and with customers, suppliers, or other third parties.

1.	2.	3.	4.	5.
Strongly Disagree	Generally Disagree	Neutral	Generally Agree	Strongly Agree

EMPOWER OTHERS

THE FIRST TWO LAWS of trust focus on personal integrity and respect for others as foundational to building a high-trust organization. But unless leaders empower team members as well, integrity and respect remain inert.

My own appreciation of empowerment took root before I was old enough to drive. I asked my dad to let me practice maneuvering the family car up and down our 100-foot-long driveway. I carefully backed our 1950 Oldsmobile out of the garage until I hit the curb, applied the brake, paused, and then accelerated again. Unfortunately, I'd forgotten to shift out of reverse. Up and over the curb I went, hanging the car up on the berm at the back of the driveway. Try though I might to get the car back on the driveway before anyone discovered my inadvertent foul-up, I could see it was hopeless. So I went back into the house and sheepishly asked my dad for help. He recruited a neighbor and we got the car back on the driveway.

Just before heading into the house, he turned, tossed the keys to me, and said, "Don't forget to put it in drive this time."

Being trusted after having failed was indelibly empowering. The recollection of my father's counterintuitive response to my humiliating first attempt at driving has given me courage to try again in situations in which my initial efforts were inadequate. More important, it has inspired me to help others when they've failed. I've often imagined "tossing the keys" to subordinates whose first efforts had landed them in a ditch. Only rarely has this leap of faith ended in a breach of trust.

It's smart to empower others. Empowering people allows them to function at their best. In organizations, our best performances are nearly always spurred on when others have empowered us—that is, trusted us with the freedom and resources to excel.

Google's Thomas Williams, a senior engineering director, offers a great example of grassroots empowerment. Rather than watching people get mired in repetitive, hamster-wheel tasks, he gives them the autonomy, as he puts it, to "build their own treadmills." Individuals are granted the leeway to experiment, innovate, set their own pace. That way, he says, "No one's telling you you're not going fast enough—everyone is telling themselves that. If you work with great people, everyone is setting their treadmill high." This kind of respectful empowerment leads to creative risk-taking, boosting the chance that people will enjoy their jobs, which in turn will benefit the whole organization.

Trust-rich organizations expect people to become their best—to concentrate more on fairness than legality, more on sharing than advantage, more on action than analysis, and more on the future than the past. With these enabling attitudes come the authority to act and the requirement for mutual trust.

At Room & Board, a national retailer of home furnishings, employees are trusted to set their own measures and priorities for performance instead of the usual managerial review most companies use. Three times a year, employees meet with management to formally discuss progress. That focus on individual goals results in more getting done.

Room & Board also trusts workers to plan their own employee events such as cookouts, sundae parties, and a day at the ballpark. It may not seem like much, but allowing the team its own way of celebrating—rather than dictating it from the top—lets people know they're empowered. Consistent with the spirit of empowerment, Room & Board doesn't even have a formal policy for sick leave or personal time off.

Some companies have no vacation limit at all. At Virgin, employees can take as much vacation as they want. The only caveat: Make sure your job gets done and the business isn't affected. ZocDoc, The Motley Fool, SurveyMonkey, LinkedIn, and others have followed suit. HubSpot, a marketing and sales firm, describes its vacation policy as "two weeks to infinity." Says Virgin founder Richard Branson, "Treat people as human beings, give them that flexibility, and I don't think they'll abuse it." At Netflix, founder Reed Hastings mocks "accounting rig-marole" and corporate metabolism fixated on control, instead opting to empower his employees. In summer 2015, Netflix announced that employees with a new child would be entitled to as much as a year off, no questions asked.

Of course, in high-performance environments there's al-ways the possibility that a lack of structure will generate stress and result in less time off, especially if the guy in the next cu-bicle never seems to take a break. Evernote, whose business is archiving and note-taking technology, tries to solve the work-aholic syndrome by giving employees $1,000 in spending money when they take off at least one full week per year. FullContact, which organizes all your contacts in the cloud, goes a step further. Its annual paid vacation includes not only your regular salary but an additional $7,500 when you take off. The deal has three conditions: You really have to go some-where; you must not check emails, texts, or voice mail; and you can't sneak in work some other way. Quirky, a consumer-goods manufacturer, engineers time off by shutting down the com-pany for one week three times a year.

Having workers so committed to the mission that you have to force them to take time off is a nice problem to have. By contrast, trust-poor organizations struggle with giving their teams the latitude to do much of anything. Wary of everybody, they often don't trust anybody, including even their most trust-worthy people. Instead, they rely on compliance committees and tattler rewards to prevent rulebreaking. This suspicious atmosphere suffocates creativity and worst of all it stifles the potential for trust to become the operative system governing behavior.

Mistrustful organizations are preoccupied with keeping people from doing their worst, while high-trust organizations focus on empowering people to do their best. Neither trust nor power should be bestowed willy-nilly. As in any area of life, trust should be granted to people with the character and competence to make responsible use of the authority with which you have entrusted them. But everyone should have the opportunity to earn your trust. The results in both morale and productivity don't take long to show up. But it may require courage on your part to take the small leaps of trust that get the ball rolling.

Long ago, my barely teen daughter approached me with a request I fervently wanted to deny: she wanted to go to a dance with a boy. My wife and I had clearly (or so I thought) established a family rule that our kids needed to be a certain age before dating. Going to a dance with a boy was a close-enough approximation to dating that I figured I could invoke the rule and that would be that. To show how much I trusted her, I told her, "I know you'll make the 'right' decision" and "I trust you to make the call." I was confident that having so overtly empowered her and having reminded her of my unalloyed trust, surely she'd not let me down. I'd get the benefit of showing trust without the risk of actually risking trust. How new I was to this phase of parenting!

I was genuinely stunned when she came back within minutes, thanking me for permission to go to the dance with the young fellow. Her choice meant that I now had my own important choice to make: overrule her judgment and thereby make the indelible point that I didn't really trust her after all, or support a decision with which I didn't agree. I opted for the latter, nervously telling her I was certain she was mature enough to decide what was right. It all worked out. She felt trusted and determined not to let me down. I felt nervous but committed to making an empowering "deposit" in what I hoped would be an ever-escalating granting of trust.

If the covenant is clear, most people will honor it, but the first leap of trust is always the most harrowing. It requires planting the seed and watching as an always-fragile seedling takes root. And frequent nurturing is a must for the initially delicate bet to grow into full-blown reciprocal trust. Empowering people whose ability to perform you're not 100 percent sure about has to start somewhere. I've learned to take baby steps before people have proven themselves, empowering them in small increments, and assessing their character and competence as I grant them authority.

Here are six ideas for empowering people to do their best work:

1 **Assume the best.** Allow people a chance to prove they can take on more responsibility. If you only grant leeway to those who've already demonstrated they can handle it, you'll

never discover new talent. A leader who trusts others to grow—knowing they may trip up—exhibits a level of trust that inspires the best in people and can ignite sparks of trust in an otherwise mistrustful environment. Identifying and empowering the most competent, highest-integrity team members is a great way to start.

2 **Be action-oriented.** Stanford's innovative D-School— the School of Design—teaches a "bias towards action." Tom Peters was famous for the line "Ready, Fire, Aim" in his 1982 book *In Search of Excellence.* This notion suggests a preference for trying out ideas rather than sitting around planning and analyzing. In short, when people are actually doing things, iterating and refining as they go, they tend to get the best results. Empowering teams to act means missteps are less expensive and people learn faster. In some ways, "taking action" is the cousin of "betting on people." Both involve a gamble. But the risk of failure is surpassed by the potential gain when done in small pilot projects with the expectation of regular project "sunsetting"—the automatic shutdown of a pilot unless specifically renewed.

3 **Forget the past.** Many organizations do things because "that's the way they've always been done." An organization's "best practices" are often just the codification of long-forgotten mistakes. High-trust organizations don't rely blindly on old rules. Instead, they trust their teams to figure out new,

more relevant ones. Empower teams to come up with their own norms.

4 **Expect foul-ups.** Granting trust doesn't guarantee perfect results. Inherent in trusting team members with authority is understanding that even the best efforts can falter. When that happens, the team should examine the reasons for the misstep, distill the lessons, and move forward with renewed vigor. Nobody aims to fail, but there's a very good reason why failure is more readily countenanced, even embraced, in Silicon Valley. While there may be a fetish in Valley culture about failure—there have even been live events like Startup Failure and FailCon to celebrate it—entrepreneurs show wisdom in recognizing that failure may fertilize the next success. Failure is often not the opposite of success but a preamble to it. (Most would agree that it was Steve Jobs's failure at NeXT that prepared him for his triumphal return to Apple.) The only true failure is that of character or effort.

Amy Edmondson, a professor at Harvard Business School, has differentiated between good failures and bad ones. "Every child learns at some point that admitting failure means taking the blame," she wrote in "Strategies for Learning from Failure" in *Harvard Business Review*. When she interviewed various executives, she found they were torn. "How can we respond constructively to failures without giving rise to an anything-goes attitude? If people aren't blamed for failures, what will ensure that they try as hard as possible to do their best work?" The way out of this "false dichotomy," according to Edmondson, is to distinguish between causes that involve blameworthy conduct—for example, abject deviance or inattention—and mistakes born of complexity or intelligence—for example, experimentation with design or process.

Trusting others means accepting that failure may well happen. Trusting others means not instantly playing what Edmondson calls "the blame game."[1] That MO winds up making people even more distrustful. As Fernando Flores and Robert Solomon warned in the article "Creating Trust" in *Business Ethics Quarterly*, "Employees can usually tell when the 'empowerment' they receive like a gift is actually a noose with which to hang themselves, a setup for blame for situations which they cannot really control."[2]

Stanford psychologist Carol Dweck has done decades of research on the motivation and productivity that come from what she calls a "growth mindset." She concludes that those who have been taught to see missteps as only a bump in the road to success, rather than an evaluation of their fixed potential, develop a love of learning, a sense of adventure, and the resilience that provide the basis for growth. Low-trust organizations document assessments rather than developing talent through progressive trust.[3]

5   **Eschew the paraphernalia of paranoia.** Focus on freeing people to do their best rather than fixating on preventing people from doing their worst. Whenever possible,

toss the thick policy manuals, especially when they're about trivial matters. End the practice of paying employees to turn in their colleagues. Stop monitoring everything they do. Such practices give rise to an anxious mindset that erodes confidence and stifles ingenuity. Nordstrom's employee handbook is a single card that reads, "Use good judgment in all situations." If you've established a covenant of trust, your confidence in your employees will turn into confidence in themselves and from there to greater achievement, better service to customers, and a higher return to shareholders.

6 **Remember that accountability is the requisite companion to empowerment.** If power and accountability are separated, mistrust and politics emerge. I once gave an assistant the responsibility to make sure I was on time and prepared for various meetings in my schedule, but I didn't give her the power to change my calendar. Soon my schedule was a mess. Only when I also turned over my scheduling could accountability follow empowerment.

FOR SOME LEADERS, THE idea of trusting employees enough to share power feels risky. These leaders have never learned the exquisite truth that giving up power is the key to creating a powerful organization. In many organizations, those with the best information do not work at headquarters, but on the front lines. Failing to trust anyone outside the executive inner circle means losing out to high-trust counterparts who marshal talent and experience from deep within the ranks, building broader coalitions and deeper coherence within the team as a whole.

A final note about empowering, trust, and integrity: Warren Buffett said, "If you lose money for the firm, I will be understanding. If you lose our reputation, I will be ruthless." To empower does not give license to breach the values entrusted to each employee as a member of the team.

Empowerment without a clear commitment to values and mission leads to organizational anarchy and ruin. We'll next see how the freedom that comes with empowerment requires a concomitant accountability for trust to thrive.

. . .

KEY QUESTION

LAW 3: EMPOWERMENT. My organization encourages me to be innovative and to take calculated risks without fearing unfair shame or punishment.

1.	2.	3.	4.	5.
Strongly Disagree	Generally Disagree	Neutral	Generally Agree	Strongly Agree

MEASURE WHAT YOU WANT TO ACHIEVE

PRESIDENT HARRY TRUMAN FAMOUSLY kept a sign on his Oval Office desk that read THE BUCK STOPS HERE! What most people don't remember is the other half of the message. The side facing the president read I'M FROM MISSOURI. A native of the Show-Me State, Truman knew that when you've been entrusted with power, you're accountable for how you use it. That meant "showing" results—and never passing "the buck." Harry Truman made accountability a political brand.

Trust grows when expectations are unambiguous. People need to know what winning looks like and where they stand on the path to victory. Trust comes with a scoreboard, with clarity around how results will be measured. Having no gauges is a setup for confusion. When people know what they're expected to achieve, they can focus on doing it rather than trying to figure out what matters most. They can trust the system.

If a basketball coach is focusing on offense, the metric will lean toward the points his team puts on the board. If he's concentrating on defense, the measure will lean toward how many points the other team scores. The respective emphases are not the same, and both are different from simply saying, "Play your best." Neither one is objectively better; a coach's choice of what to emphasize will depend on the skills of the players and his expectation of what will lead to victory. Depending on the opponent, the coach can reinforce offense or defense. Without clarity, a freelancing or bewildered player is disconnected from the game plan and becomes a liability.

You don't have to be a student of the NBA to recognize that any number of teams had star individuals who were unable to lead their teams anywhere, while some NBA teams were great not because of one great player but because several players worked together under an accountability system established by the coach. The San Antonio Spurs of 2014, the New York Knicks of 1970 (and plenty of champions in between) won titles because each player was accountable to a system. As with basketball, companies perform best when expectations are clear, where roles are focused, and where teammates can rely on each other. In that environment, trust can develop and reliable interdependencies can flourish.

Salesforce, for example, has institutionalized accountability. Chairman and co-CEO Marc Benioff created V2MOM to give the company a "high level of organizational alignment and communication while growing at breakneck speeds."

V2MOM, an acronym for Vision, Values, Methods, Obstacles, and Measures, makes accountability a hallmark for the company and for each employee. V2MOM establishes a total alignment around the measures by which people can be held accountable. "Vision" lays out what you aim to do. "Values" describes what's important about that vision—articulating the principles and beliefs that guided it. "Methods" identifies the steps needed to get the job done by everyone, whereas "Obstacles" describes what stands in the way. "Measures" provide a metric to let people know when the vision had been attained. According to Benioff, V2MOM guides every decision at Salesforce and gives a "detailed map of where we were going, as well as a compass to direct us there."

Here are four suggestions for creating a culture in which trust is secured by accountability:

1 **Define what winning looks like.** It's easier to succeed when we have a sense of what we're trying to achieve. Without clarity about outcomes, nobody can be accountable. Leaders need to start with a clear vision everyone can remember—not only with budgets and time frames but also with specific results team members own. It's not enough to set vague goals, no matter how elevated—We Want to Be Number One—if there's no way to measure results. Without sufficiently sharp definition, accountability can't live. Without accountability, trust erodes.

Some years ago, FranklinCovey conducted a survey of thousands of employees across multiple industries showing that trust levels weren't very high in most companies. That conclusion correlated with the inability of employees, even leaders, to articulate the central goals of their respective enterprises. In one telling case, nine top executives were asked to list their company's top three objectives. The tally: twenty-four different goals.

It's little wonder team members don't really trust what they're being told if the targets are ever-moving, hazy, or entirely unknown. Clarity empowers people; ambiguity cripples them. And without clarity around winning, it's hard to set up the scoreboard around measures of accountability.

2 **Set clear expectations.** Say you're given authority to build a new facility and you're responsible for its timely, cost-effective completion. Now imagine that no one gives you a budget, a timetable, a list of aesthetic requirements, or any other measure that helps assess your work. You proudly get the building done in eighteen months for $40 million, only to learn that the people who had "empowered" you expected it six months sooner and $10 million cheaper. You had the power. You took responsibility. But no one set up accountability criteria. That's the kind of pseudo empowerment that ends careers and destroys companies. Unfortunately, in many organizations, the trio of power, responsibility, and accountability get separated. This leaves no one fully empowered and no one fully accountable. In this vacuum, trust withers.

3 **Expect accountability to enhance trust.** Many leaders are only too happy to give team members the power to carry out all kinds of mini-assignments and contributory tasks. But that's not enough to harness the power of trust or the accountability that accompanies it. Unless people are also given responsibility for big-picture outcomes, they know leaders don't trust them with the important stuff. On the other hand, if leaders are willing to collaborate with team members on the overall objectives, most team members will rise to the challenge, feeling trusted with outcomes, not just tasks.

4 **Accompany accountability with credit.** When team members succeed in achieving broader objectives, the best leaders step aside and allow them to take the glory. And if teams stumble, the most trustworthy leaders step in to absorb the blame. (Players take the wins; coaches take the losses.) Nothing kills trust faster than a leader who calls shots and makes assignments, only to blame everyone else when things go wrong. Trust wilts in the presence of leaders who absorb the limelight. It grows when they reflect it on their team members.

IF YOU HAVEN'T SPENT much time in a high-trust environment, accountability may initially feel like mistrust. Some people might ask, "Is it really trust if you're constantly asked to account for the power you've been granted?" The answer is yes. To prosper, organizational trust has to be protected from misuse. Without accountability, trust doesn't have a chance. But like the image of pulling up carrots to see if they're still growing, too frequent measures will kill trust and arrest growth. High-trust accountability should be about removing obstacles rather than citing failures. It should feel less like doling out blame and more like people paying attention and, then, celebrating successes.

There's no point in trusting individuals if what they do with our trust doesn't come close to what we expect. Conversely, it's no good being trusted if we're not sure what we're supposed to do with another's trust. If we don't have a clear sense of responsibility for outcomes, we may lose trust altogether, even when we act in good faith.

Accountability illuminates trust and makes empowerment work by giving people the clarity and confidence they need to be trustworthy in meeting objectives and the knowledge that they'll be given credit for success.

. . .

KEY QUESTION

LAW 4: MEASURES. In my organization I trust the processes by which my work is evaluated.

1.	2.	3.	4.	5.
Strongly Disagree	Generally Disagree	Neutral	Generally Agree	Strongly Agree

CREATE A COMMON DREAM

I MAGINE WINNING. SEE VIVIDLY in your mind's eye what success looks like, then let that vision animate your entire team. Tackling challenges on the journey to a common goal is a natural way for team members to come to trust one another. On the other hand, failing to articulate a common dream or a vision of success almost ensures finger-pointing when the inevitable setbacks occur.

At the world-class level, a hairbreadth often separates the gold-medal winner from the runner-up. Many Olympians, even in events that focus on individual performance—sprints, weightlifting, diving—say that trusting teammates and coaches to achieve a common goal accounted in large part for their ability to make the sacrifices required to achieve their dreams.

Olympians describe being driven through long hours of training and deprivation by imagining a place on the medals stand. A team of twelve-year-old baseball players dreams of winning a Little League World Series trophy. A triathlete envisions crossing the finish line to a loudspeaker blaring, "You *are* an Ironman!" And a jockey, an owner, and a horse trainer imagine joining forces to win the Kentucky Derby.

Athletic dreams are most inspiring when they're more than a generalized hope for success. It's the same with organizational objectives. The most effective ones are tangible images that help people push through inevitable disappointments. While organizational visions may not be as vivid as the image of a spot on the podium, they should be tangible.

Keep these six ideas in mind as you create and refine an overarching vision, mission, or dream:

1 **Make your mission inclusive.** All organizations have multiple constituencies, including employees, customers, investors, and communities served. Articulating a purpose that brings these constituencies together is a good starting point for organizational vision. The goal is to find something of consequence that all stakeholders can root for. Consider again the vision of a team in the Olympics. Winning a medal is a goal everyone can get behind, from the athletes and their families to the coaches, the fans, and even the sponsors.

Many leaders limit the mission of public companies to maximizing profits or growing at a particular rate. But profits and growth are not missions; profits are the result of delivering something customers want at a price that represents real value to them. The mission is to uniquely serve customers and create value. Those are goals people can trust. If you come up with a mission like the one Olympic athletes use to inspire their quest for gold, profits and growth should follow. Today's information workers are volunteers—they want to own the reason for their labor.

2 **Having a mission means more than having a mission statement.** We've all seen executive-crafted mission statements, full of jargon and lofty language. Businesses like to claim they're "changing the world" thanks to "forward-thinking products" and "unimpeachable integrity." What companies frequently miss is that attempts at being aspirational and inspirational can come off as interchangeable and irrelevant—and in the worst case, can create cynicism.

Unless your mission statement expresses unique ways people can be (1) respected members of (2) a winning team (3) doing something meaningful, you may as well go to the online Mission Statement Generator, where you can combine an adverb, an adjective, a noun, and a conjunction with an opener and a closer to yield a meaningless mission statement.

Make sure your team participates in generating the statement, and make sure it is around what the organization actually does. In other words, make the process participatory and the outcome specific. Recognize, too, that a mission statement does not guarantee a mission. Many trust-poor organizations have mission statements that exclude significant stakeholders.

Crafting a coherent, ambitious, and realistic mission brings many stakeholders together, allowing each to contribute color, texture, and meaning. The very process of talking about mission can help stamp out the political maneuvering and mistrust among stakeholders that would otherwise fill the natural vacuum of a missionless organization. And that process should create a podium on which everyone in the organization can stand.

3 **Collect and celebrate "hero stories."** People tend to think inductively—that is, from the specific to the general. The anecdote tells the larger tale and animates the mission for everyone. Journalists use stories of individuals to explain complex issues. So do presidents during State of the Union addresses, in which they point up to the gallery and call out the soldier who rescued a brother on the battlefield. Part of reinforcing a mission is honoring those in the organization who advance its overarching goals.

"Hero stories" can provide a powerful example of an organization's vision in action. In *Heroes: What They Do and Why We Need Them*, Scott Allison and George Goethals provide a thoughtful, well-researched survey on the psychology of heroes in both history and fiction. Portraits of such characters as Lincoln, Churchill, Mandela, Margaret Thatcher, Ernest Shackleton—even Rick Blaine in *Casablanca*—illustrate the connection between heroism and leadership.[1]

JetBlue collects stories of crewmembers who go the extra mile for customers. To remind everyone of the mission of "bringing humanity back to air travel," I've opened board meetings by reading compelling letters from grateful customers.

I recall giving talks every year at Trammell Crow Company about employees who personified our values. One year I decided to change my stump speech, leaving out one of the more colorful stories everyone had already heard about a partner who had gone the extra mile for a client. In more than one city, people came up to me afterward to grumble, "You forgot to tell the story about how one partner delighted a tenant!" Clearly, everyone already knew the story, yet they wanted to hear it again. Call it company folklore. There's a reason stories of individual team members exemplifying the values of the organization in achieving its mission become institutional memory. Members of high-trust teams love these tangible reminders of "why we're different."

4   **Replace an aging vision.** As organizations grow, the big picture tends to blur. Early passions fade. Bureaucracies emerge. People are less eager to come to work if they don't know what they're working toward, or if they sense the enterprise has not refreshed its purpose. When NBA commissioner Adam Silver in summer 2015 redrew the league's long-standing and too-long mission statement, he elevated it to a "calling." Silver framed the NBA's role through a more expansive—and inclusive—lens that would inspire the league's followers to "compete with intensity, lead with integrity, and inspire play."

If you can no longer express your organization's vision in a simple, irresistible way, you've probably drifted off track. That means it's time to refocus—not just the vision but also the organization itself. The goal: Every member of the team should have a direct line of sight to the podium.

5 **Don't think small—do think simple.** Pick a goal that the team will be proud to achieve. Whether it's building a new product or serving a community in need, individuals want tangible objectives to move toward, not vague problems to maneuver away from. If the goal is just to avoid a bad outcome, the results of any sacrifice required to achieve the dream will be less motivating and less likely to result in enduring trust among colleagues.

As a leader, keep your team focused on a clear, compelling, and limited set of big goals—ideally, no more than three. You should be the guardian and evangelist of your organization's priorities; it's up to you to keep them in neon letters so all employees can see what you're all about. At Microsoft, for decades that meant putting "a computer on every desk and in every home." Amazon began with the goal to offer "every book, ever printed, in any language, all available in less than 60 seconds." Pepsi famously wanted to "Beat Coke." JetBlue was founded with a mission to bring humanity back to air travel. Churchill's "V" sign during World War II was the symbol of his single-minded objective: victory.

6   **Expect great dreams to require sacrifice.** It's difficult to imagine a meaningful dream without some level of sacrifice. People make sacrifices in all successful organizations, in all healthy relationships, at every stage of life. In most functional families, bonds grow and strengthen precisely because so much is required—and given. We tend to love those things for which, and people for whom, we've sacrificed. So if you want to achieve a meaningful outcome, don't be afraid of sacrifice. But the dream must be one leaders are willing to sacrifice for as well. The novelist Peter Beagle put it nicely (if a bit graphically) in *The Last Unicorn*: "Real magic can never be made by offering someone else's liver. You must tear out your own, and not expect to get it back."[2]

Fortunately, the kinds of sacrifices required have intrinsic benefits. But remember that asking for sacrifice is not a "technique" to build trust. Life in organizations is not a blind-trust exercise in which you ask people to follow you into a dense forest. Instead, you're asking people to give of themselves for something they believe in.

When you've got the dream right, people commit to its achievement in ways that will surprise you. Young entrepreneurs will forgo a normal social life, locking themselves in the proverbial garage to gain the hundreds of extra hours they need to build a product the world doesn't yet have. And when it comes to a family's mission, parents will give up valuable midcareer time to be closer to their growing kids.

Naturally, the topic of sacrifice feels a bit risky when creating a common dream. No matter your own sacrifices, you don't want to be a slave driver or demand more than people can reasonably give. But if you have integrity, if you show respect, if you offer responsibility and take it yourself, if you show what the mile markers are, and if the vision is clear and widely held, you'll be surprised at the sacrifices people will be willing to make. If people trust their leaders, their colleagues, and themselves, they'll be more than willing to take the extra risk, to stay the extra hour, to sacrifice the routine for the remarkable.

One dramatic example: Starbucks had enjoyed years of breakneck expansion when Howard Schultz retired as its CEO in 2000. But within a few years, Schultz emailed his successor, as well as senior management, to lament the "commoditization of our brand" and "the watering down of the Starbucks experience." In early 2008, with the company in a potential death spiral and takeover vultures hovering, Schultz decided to return as CEO, and he called for sacrifice.[3]

With both the earnestness and the bravado he'd become known for, he used sacrifice as a way to get everyone's attention. He quickly shut down eight hundred underperforming US stores, letting go four thousand employees. Some long-standing and cherished benefits were cut back. Other steps were less structural but dramatic nonetheless. For three and a half hours, at a cost of $6 million in lost revenue, all Starbucks stores closed so baristas could be retrained at the espresso machine.

At the end of it all, and at a cost of some $30 million, Schultz brought ten thousand store managers together in New

Orleans for a weeklong pep rally and to put in fifty thousand hours of community service for Hurricane Katrina cleanup. In relatively short order, Starbucks turned around to reclaim its position as a beloved brand and a valued place to work. Although the company's pivot was not, of course, solely due to Schultz's immediate moves (nor was it without challenges), his call was an overall repositioning of Starbucks's internal culture, as well as its public image. At a low point, shared sacrifice pulled the Starbucks team together, and the returning Schultz reestablished a trust that had ebbed during his absence. The common dream was restored and trust levels increased.

MOST PEOPLE WANT TO feel they're working toward a goal that is concrete, important, and lasting—not just working their way through a series of repetitive tasks. Trust is far more likely to develop when a shared dream brings each member of the team together in pursuit of something meaningful, especially when they have shaped and therefore own it. (I've even seen teams in turnarounds band together around things like "losing less money this month than we lost last.")

When people can rally around a common goal, reaching for a summit that's consistent with their values, they'll sacrifice together, lift each other's burdens, and do their utmost not to let each other down. Such are the characteristics of high-trust organizations that follow the laws of trust in pursuit of a common dream.

Perhaps the most vivid example of creating a common dream can be found in a talk given by Anson Dorrance, the longtime head coach of women's soccer at the University of North Carolina. He's one of the most successful athletic leaders in history, guiding UNC to twenty-two national championships. In a revealing video clip at www.whatdriveswinning.com, he talks about his team "playing for something bigger than themselves"—"for the person on their left, the person on their right, the person behind, and the person in front of them." Dorrance explains that if his team reaches the national championship game, he spends that weekend "writing a letter to every senior on my roster thanking her for the incredible human contribution she's made to my team."

Before the big game, he hands out the letters to the seniors, then asks them to leave the locker room. He reads photocopies of the letters to the remaining players to show the "extraordinary human beings" they're playing for. One such senior was Caroline Boneparth, the daughter of Peter Boneparth, with whom I serve on the JetBlue board. (Caroline allowed her letter to be included in *Coaching Wisdom*, a recent book about athletic leaders, so the letter isn't private anymore.) Nicknamed "Care" by the coach, Caroline wasn't a star. She rarely played. But she was a captain nonetheless. In his letter to her, Dorrance wrote that Caroline was "both steel and velvet. This is you. You are so strong and sweet and I cherish you for it. Thank you for taking 'care' of everyone for four wonderful years. I am going to miss you." Who would not be inspired to play their hardest for Caroline? Who would not want to be led by Anson Dorrance?

.   .   .

KEY QUESTION

LAW 5: VISION. When I think of the most important thing my organization aims to do, I feel a sense of pride.

1.	2.	3.	4.	5.
Strongly Disagree	Generally Disagree	Neutral	Generally Agree	Strongly Agree

KEEP EVERYONE INFORMED

To build and maintain trust, a leader must communicate. Leaders must be determined to share the facts with everyone, simply, persuasively, and thoroughly. That means telling it like it is, during good times and bad.

In low-trust organizations, communication is generally wanting. We may know what's going on in our department, but when it comes to the company's broader goals, we're in the dark. Left to guess, we begin to wonder if leaders have a real plan. An inspiring mission becomes an impossibility, and we begin to wonder whether we've got the respect of those in the executive suite. From there, trust goes downhill.

Academic studies have shown that employee satisfaction depends significantly on effective internal communication. Team members have a hard time developing trust in their leaders if they're unsure where the overall organization is headed and whether that direction is good for them. The solution to this trust-killing lack of information is, of course, communication and lots of it. "Err on the side of overcommunication," Max De Pree, the renowned leader of Herman Miller office furniture, liked to say.

Trust-building organizations tell the truth, through words and actions and words again. They report unpleasant news as openly as they celebrate success. People are smart. They pick up on spin as well as on partial truths and legalisms. If you came out with a new flavor of soft drink that bombed, say so and be clear about what your team is doing to fix the problem. If you have to lay people off, don't do it secretly, hoping competitors and the media won't notice. Take responsibility for your decision while helping people understand its implications. And don't hire corporate "bad guys" to do the dirty work.

While transparency takes on different forms, the common characteristic of each is a commitment to trust the team with information. Some examples:

- Autodesk, maker of architectural and engineering software, aims to be totally transparent about its financial results. Each quarter, executives "share the numbers" with all employees by inviting them to listen in on the earnings call.
- Several years ago, SC Johnson, the household cleaning-supplies titan, distributed a fifty-page summary of its business goals to all employees, taking the risk that a copy might be leaked.

- Google developed a "bureaucracy busters" program in which employees were asked to post ideas for cutting through internal red tape. Almost twelve hundred ideas emerged, including better maps of Google's campuses.
- In 2012, Kimberly-Clark hosted a "One K-C Culture Jam" for employees worldwide. "Transcending organizational and geographical silos," a five-day online event produced ideas not only for better Kleenex but also for improving the culture.
- Zappos, the online shoe retailer, made transparency a calling. In what commentators called "revolutionary," the organization decided some years back it would share its sales data with everybody in the supply chain—tweets from the CEO linked to internal emails about facility operations. Which sneakers were selling and which hiking boots were not? What were the margins and what were the inventories? Employees and customers got the information, but so, too, did competitors. The theory: Transparency would generate trust and loyalty in multiple constituencies. It's too soon to know if Zappos's transparency produced measurable results—and the company has had high turnover of late due to other management issues—but it won praise in the business press for its transparency on sales.

Here are four communication principles that will build trust:

1 **Own the bad news.** Few of us are eager to confront error or unfortunate circumstances beyond our control. But whether it's a hiring decision gone awry or unexpected market forces or the expectation that the US Food and Drug Administration might not approve the drug a key division has been developing, people want to know the bad news right along with the good. If people are told only the good, no matter how triumphantly, they will be consumed by mistrust: What aren't they telling me? Does doom wait just around the corner? Sugarcoating the bad, or ignoring it altogether, is a common mistake we've all made.

It's tempting to believe that downplaying bad tidings will lessen their negative impact, but evidence suggests it only exacerbates the impact. When the real story comes out, you'll have a hard time explaining why you weren't up front with your team. It's far better to get out ahead of the news and use the setback as an opportunity to build trust by showing respect for your colleagues. To be sure, most organizations with competent crisis-management and PR teams can minimize weak spots—and too many do little else. But most people prefer to be associated with a company in which leaders aren't afraid to tell the truth.

The truth has many clear benefits. The most obvious: The more transparent you are about challenges, the more likely it is that individuals will come up with creative approaches to conquer them. If yours is a company employees are proud of— where they believe they're respected and where they own the mission—then they'll be much more inclined to stick around and help instead of fleeing at the first sign of trouble.

2 **Discipline yourself to stay positive.** This isn't the same thing as glossing over the truth. Staying positive means that when the going gets tough, good leaders steer clear of negativity, high-velocity language, and tantrums. We've all had moments in which disappointment, embarrassment, and stress combined to produce a cocktail of negative feeling. Adrenaline is natural. But we also know that it's wiser to let such feelings pass before we talk to colleagues, write emails, or call a meeting. Even one tirade by a leader can endure, and carelessly written emails seem to live forever. The trust that develops slowly can be lost evermore in a rant.

From childhood, Dwight Eisenhower had an awful temper. It's not that he outgrew it to become the moderate, smiling Ike we see in the newsreels. Instead, he learned to master his temper. He wrote down the names of those he despised, then tore up the pieces of paper and tossed them "into the lowest drawer of my desk." That, he explained, "finishes the incident and so far as I'm concerned, that fellow." Yes, like most of us, Eisenhower occasionally raged—but in solitude.

3 **Pay attention to body language and atmospherics.** Research indicates that gestures and facial expressions are potent forms of communication. The way you sit, how much you fidget, and whether you're making eye contact—all

of these send subtle messages. An eye roll, an arm cross, or a finger wag will turn off listeners, and averting eye contact or looking down when speaking will suggest indifference. Pay attention to your body language and cultivate the habit of listening to capture what the other person is saying.

Whether they know it or not, organizations also communicate a great deal symbolically. How people dress, where executives eat and entertain, what art is displayed—they all matter. These forms of communication can separate people or bring them together. When you're outside your organization, be on the lookout for how other companies do things and which practices are consistent with the culture you're trying to develop. On the inside, be alert for dated practices and scrap them when they do more harm than good. At Peterson Partners, the investment firm I founded twenty years ago, we scrapped the artwork and replaced it with an array of logotypes, scale models, and other memorabilia of the products and advertisements celebrating the hundred and fifty portfolio companies we've backed. This reminds people that we work for our entrepreneurs.

When it comes to nonverbal communication, nothing trumps a leader's actions. Whether kind or ruthless, actions at the top say it all. There are some actions everyone notices, such as in a companywide presentation or in certain personnel decisions. But there are many more actions few see, and those often count just as much. Word gets around about how you behave on the tennis court or when you pull into your parking space. As a team leader, your credibility rests disproportionately on the many small decisions you make every day. Even if most people don't witness these, they'll feel them—in the same way we often can feel comfortable or agitated without fully knowing why.

You are communicating, whether or not you want to. So be intentional: Think about building trust with each word and action.

4 **Consider what budgets say about your priorities.** Realize that your budget is among your firm's most reliable indicators of its values. If people find themselves on a team that can't budget in ways that sync up with the team's values, trust dissolves; if you're going to emphasize work-life balance as a priority but budget so as to be chronically understaffed, employees will sense a lack of integrity. You're better off saying nothing than saying one thing and budgeting for another.

Keeping budgets secret often lets people get away with obscuring problems. The problems, of course, don't disappear. They just linger and intensify before erupting. But while transparency in budgeting makes low-trust organizations nervous, their high-trust counterparts have learned that the late US Supreme Court Justice Louis Brandeis had it right: sunshine is a superb disinfectant. Because budgets are compelling value statements at the very heart of developing trust, they must be open.

Radical openness is a concept coined a few years ago by author-consultants Don Tapscott and Anthony Williams. In a

2013 book, they explained the phenomenon—both its foundation and its utility. "Times have changed," they wrote. "While secrecy and opacity have been hallmarks of business behavior in the past, maintaining and defending secrets is costly and difficult in an era where billions of smartphone-wielding citizens can transmit information around the globe in a heartbeat."[1]

The extension of radical openness, Williams explained in a TED Blog Q&A, means that industries "are opening up their innovation processes and treating their customers and partners as valuable sources of intelligence and new ideas." Rather than fighting to "protect proprietary resources and innovations," companies share intellectual property "in a bid to accelerate research, cultivate relationships and stimulate progress in other areas where they will see profits."[2] In the spirit of openness, when Warren Buffett bought a private plane at Berkshire Hathaway (which could afford it and which had a leader whose time was particularly valuable), he wryly named it *The Indefensible*.

In this spirit of openness, high-trust leaders think of a budget as values in action and budgeting as, literally, an investment in trust. Sharing budgets broadly is a great way to debate priorities and build trust over time.

THE INTEGRITY OF LEADERS is the *sine qua non* for a high-trust culture, and communication—through words, symbols, budgets, and stories—is the fuel they use to power trust in their organizations. Leaders should thus avoid the trust-destroying silence, secrecy, and doublespeak so damaging to organizations. By learning to communicate lavishly, open up budgets for discussion, and deal with good and bad news with equal openness, one can secure a reputation for trustworthiness—internally and externally.

. . .

KEY QUESTION

LAW 6: COMMUNICATION. In my organization I usually have the information I need to do my job—and when I don't, I know I can get it without being dismissed or patronized.

1.	2.	3.	4.	5.
Strongly Disagree	Generally Disagree	Neutral	Generally Agree	Strongly Agree

EMBRACE RESPECTFUL
CONFLICT

IN MOST ORGANIZATIONS, PEOPLE squabble over creative differences, turf, and budgets. They butt heads over all manner of political issues, big and small. The more people there are, the more matters they have to fuss over. It's just a fact of work—and life. The difference between conflict in a dysfunctional company and in a high-trust organization is not whether there's conflict, but how people deal with it.

There is a distinction between conflict that works and that which does not. Where debate is a pretense, it gets the organization nowhere and does more harm than good. By contrast, if the debate is truly a process whose objective is to find a good answer within an open marketplace of ideas, then it is powerfully trust building.

A standard of mutual trust and respect—where the best idea, not the most powerful presenter, wins—allows disagreement to generate better ideas. Out of high-trust discussion come not only new ideas but also more trust. And that increased trust makes debate less threatening. It's a virtuous cycle.

Steve Jobs could be gratuitously condescending and impatient. But at Apple (as noted in Law 2), his emphasis on freewheeling discussion helped the company invent game-changing products. Jobs knew that corporate consensus—choosing the middle ground, splitting the difference among competing ideas—was a formula for incrementalism, the antithesis of creativity and innovation. If Jobs had believed in that approach, we might all still be using iPods.

Robust debate prevents companies from languishing in the status quo. Just ask IBM, which didn't anticipate Microsoft. Or ask Microsoft, which didn't anticipate Google, the rise of mobile, or the rebirth of Apple.

Technological disruptions depend on debate. In *The Creative Priority: Driving Innovative Business in the Real World*, industrial designer Jerry Hirshberg (Nissan cars, TaylorMade golf clubs) coined the concept of creative abrasion. "Friction between individuals and groups is typically thought of as something harmful," he wrote. "Creative abrasion recognizes the positive dimensions of friction, the requisite role it plays in making things go. Without it, engines would not work; a crucial source of heat and electricity would be eliminated." What the best organizations do, according to Hirschberg, is recognize and transform "pregnant moments of friction and collision into opportunities for breakthroughs."[1]

To outsiders, an organization with creative abrasion may appear to be conflict ridden. But inside, leaders know they're harnessing different viewpoints to power progress. As in most functional human relationships, people in high-performing organizations work through friction in a spirit of mutual respect. When opposing points of view are contested freely, the result is often an outside-the-box solution. Being proactive in dealing with differences, though uncomfortable, roots out fuzzy thinking, faulty practices, and political maneuvering. It can accustom people to working through differences instead of working at cross-purposes, and it only happens when a level of trust has already taken hold. Facing conflict requires courage. As Peter Drucker wrote, "Whenever you see a successful business, someone once made a courageous decision." Many times, courageous leadership means not running from problems. When trust is strained, people avoid the pain of dealing with problems. Instead, they keep their mouths shut or take half measures—or simply run away.

But in a high-trust organization, people run toward the fire rather than just hoping it will put itself out or that someone else will handle it. After all, it's their own house that's at risk, built through years of overcoming challenges, winning, and celebrating with people they like and trust. I recently served as a board member of Ladder Capital Finance, a commercial real estate investment business. It was founded by Brian Harris, whose father was a Brooklyn firefighter. Brian's father indelibly taught his son, "If you see a fire, run *toward* it, not away from it"—and I've tried to adopt that worldview.

Let me tell you about my own biggest business mistake—an error rooted in my own failure to run toward the fire when taking responsibility might have made all the difference. In late 1986, many people in US commercial real estate—caught up in the industry's big gains at the time—failed to notice it was headed for a crash. But as a senior partner at the world's largest private real estate developer, Trammell Crow Company in Dallas, I'd had a grim premonition. The firm had more than $10 billion in leveraged real estate assets and was spending billions more each year buying and building new properties. All over the world, we had transformed skylines and landscapes, created jobs and wealth. It was a heady time, and not an easy one in which to pause and ask: How long would it be until we were careening down a mountain of debt?

We had always been driven by the credo of founder Trammell Crow, who liked to remind young partners, "In the history of the world, the seller has *always* been wrong." Most of us had grown up in a system that was allergic to selling, or even to borrowing less than we could, so we plowed ahead doing what we did best: building more skyscrapers, retail shopping centers, and warehouses. But from where I sat, we wouldn't survive unless we applied the brakes in time. I argued for serious pruning of our development activity. Eventually, my pleas to sell every nonstrategic asset conflicted so directly with Trammell's philosophy that I failed to do what I should have started with: making my case to him face-to-face.

Instead, Trammell and I tiptoed around each other—each managing the organization with our own respective agendas—until it was obvious to everyone that there was little unity at the top. By the end, I decided to leave the state, opting to commute a thousand miles every week from my home to my office in Dallas rather than squarely face the daily crisis of trust. The real estate market did in fact crash, sending the company into turmoil. Partners jumped ship, and I found myself embroiled in preventable litigation with Trammell (who had been my most important mentor), and with the company (which was now my former employer).

Though the details aren't important, failing to run toward the fire and be clear about my concerns turned out to be a watershed for me in thinking about handling mistakes and how that affects trust within an organization. My financial analysis had been solid, but I ran from the smoke that indicated the fire had already started. In the end, the whole episode may well have contributed to the eventual sale of Trammell Crow Company—not what anyone was hoping for.

My mismanagement of this conflict is, to this day, my worst professional judgment. However, I took from it a valuable lesson about the importance of confronting a difficult reality. I've learned as well that when you choose to ignore or run away from bad news, you're only doing a disservice to yourself, your colleagues, and your family—and you're violating their trust in you.

In the almost thirty years since, I've never stopped reminding myself to seek out and take on conflict, and sooner, not later. When parties disagree openly in a spirit of mutual respect and move toward—not away from—problems, trust grows rather than recedes.

You can convert discord into opportunity by facilitating these three practices:

1 **Set the standard that the best ideas win.** Any other criterion for making decisions may well be a symptom of low trust. If the best idea loses, it can mean that disagreement is so abhorred that many ideas never get aired in the first place. It could especially mean that input from junior employees or new hires is ignored. When senior management rarely accepts ideas that don't come from within its ranks, those siloed executives don't get fresh ideas. In trust-poor enterprises—which frown on debate, or even punish it—the tranquil veneer of equanimity may reign, but it's the type of quiet you might find in a hospital. Just below the surface simmers a much worse kind of disease than the fever that may result from conflict. Deprived of the information that comes from expressing disagreement along the way, such organizations allow problems to fester, with no route to needed change. The suppressed conflict always finds its way to the surface—later, and in more costly forms.

In high-trust cultures, on the other hand, leaders don't just look for employees who learn to toe the line. Quite the contrary: When great ideas come from less senior team members, high-trust leaders aim the spotlight at the unexpected contributors. That kind of celebration encourages bold thinking from all quarters. Where the best ideas win, more good ideas surface.

2 **Think like a mediator, not a judge.** An important step toward resolving differences is to make sure team mem-

bers are heard. That means being a good, neutral listener—listening without an agenda. Before offering feedback, be sure you've heard all sides. Strong leaders hold back as much as they speak up. At times, leadership can mean silence. When others are allowed to speak, trust grows.

When either party in a conflict walks away steaming with resentment, the whole organization suffers. So while you want to exercise the wisdom of a judge, aim also to reflect the attitude of a mediator: Instead of assigning fault or choosing sides, look for common ground to create win-win solutions. It may be that by seeking more viewpoints and allowing perspectives to clash, the group can settle on a solution built on diverse perspectives. Sometimes there's no way to square a circle, and it's counterproductive to try to harmonize that which is irreconcilable. But the point is to think twice before declaring an impasse, and along the way to ensure that everyone has been given a fair hearing.

3 **Don't let tensions boil over.** Suppressed strife invariably blows up. Disagreements happen. So process conflict along the way. If there's a safety valve on the pressure cooker, there won't be an explosion.

EVEN AFTER FOLLOWING SUCH counsel, it's inevitable that some conversations will end in hurt feelings. When people are invested in their ideas, they care about outcomes and put themselves on the line. But high-trust leaders realize this is a good thing and that conflict is infinitely better than apathy. Fostering a culture in which conflict is processed openly is vital not only to innovation but also to the creation of trust. But the tension must be faced squarely and discussed openly. You can't fear the fire.

Coercive leaders who quell debate, spackle over differences, or run from fires can put a temporary stop to conflict, but they have merely increased the likelihood that the superficial peace achieved will ultimately explode in trust-annihilating aggression. Moving toward the fire, on the other hand, ensures that the best ideas win and allows leaders to douse any flames that threaten the organization.

. . .

KEY QUESTION

LAW 7: CONFLICT. I can point to instances where the *best* ideas won—even though they weren't popular or endorsed by my organization's loudest or most prominent leaders.

1.	2.	3.	4.	5.
Strongly Disagree	Generally Disagree	Neutral	Generally Agree	Strongly Agree

LAW
8

SHOW HUMILITY

SELF-PROMOTING DIVAS AND POWER-HOARDING executives destroy organizational trust. High-trust leaders, on
the other hand, see their role as a stewardship—guiding people, assets, and decision making—protecting the values and
vision that make an organization what it is. And that requires
humility.

French President Charles de Gaulle—not exactly a shrink-
ing violet himself—used to remind people that "cemeteries are
full of indispensable men." Diva-style leaders who ignore that
mordant reminder of humility are unlikely to build anything
that lasts longer than they do. Only those interested in leadership as more than mere ego gratification have a chance to build
something that outlasts them.

When a CEO becomes a household name, that CEO may
well need to get his or her own house in order. In *Good to
Great*, Jim Collins lamented the trend of boards that become

"enamored with charismatic CEOs," a tendency that, he concluded, was "most damaging" for "the long-term health of companies." Indeed, his research showed that "good-to-great" CEOs generally received very little attention, whether in the mainstream press or in interviews for the book.

It's natural for strong leaders to feel they make a vital difference to everything—and everyone—in an organization. They often believe that the firm's legacy and their own are one and the same. But that kind of arrogance (*après moi le déluge*) can be deadly to trust. Leaders with a me-first attitude are often too distracted playing the smartest person in the room to realize the floodwaters have begun to rise and their entire organization is at risk. That's exactly what happened at Enron. When CEO Jeff Skilling proclaimed, "I *am* Enron," the energy giant was at its peak. Then came the tempest. By the time the floodwaters had receded, Skilling was in prison and his name synonymous with one of the largest bankruptcies in US history.

The hubris displayed by Skilling, along with founder Kenneth Lay and CFO Andrew Fastow, didn't just destroy Enron; their fatal lack of humility damaged the public's trust in business leaders in general. With a raft of scandals at WorldCom, Tyco, Global Crossing, and Adelphia Communications, as well as at Enron, it wasn't just these companies or their low-trust leaders who took the trust hit—we all did.

Not unlike the destruction of trust brought about by megalomaniacal divas is the damage Wall Street banks can cause to companies or to the economy in general, as in the 2008 melt-down. These disasters have affected popular attitudes toward our entire system of free-market capitalism. The trust of many in a system that has been the most spectacular generator of innova-tion in history was damaged by the unbridled greed of a few.

Only when leaders are grounded in humility through en-lightened self-interest can they build an enduring organiza-tion. The statement *"L'état, c'est moi,"* attributed to French King Louis XIV, isn't a sustainable governing principle. (In fact, it helped sow the seeds of the French Revolution.) Instead, hu-mility makes it possible for a leader to build for a future he won't see, ensuring that the best parts of the business not only last but also can be built on by the next generation.

Just as high-trust organizations are careful not to hire Louis XIV imitators, they also avoid treating employees like second-class citizens. As roles and reporting relationships differ, high-trust organizations figure out ways to treat with dignity those who aren't executives, lack Ivy League degrees, or go about their tasks quietly. Does the CEO view a receptionist as "help"—an anonymous face he or she walks by each morning—or as a team member with the potential to rise through the ranks buoyed by the memory of being treated well by the chief?

High-trust leaders assume all employees are on their way to great things. They may remember that Rodney McMullen, CEO at Kroger, started as a stock clerk at the local Kroger grocery store before he became its CEO thirty-six years later. Similarly, Walmart CEO Doug McMillon began as an hourly summer associate in a distribution center, unloading trucks. At Boeing, Alan Mulally was hired right out of college as an engineer and went on to become its CEO before becoming the chief executive at Ford. And Carly Fiorina reminds us that someone who's worked as a receptionist and secretary can become a CEO and presidential candidate.

It's impossible to build a high-trust organization around a caste system. While there are always different positions on a business team with different levels of responsibility, each is vital to winning. No one should feel unimportant to the mission. To build a high-trust group, a leader needs to show that everyone has value.

The importance of showing appreciation for every member of the team, as well as for the contributions of those who laid a company's groundwork, was exemplified by William A. Hewitt at John Deere. After a century of dominance by International Harvester (IH) in the farm-machinery industry, competitor John Deere got a new president in Hewitt, a dropout from Harvard Business School who married the great-great-granddaughter of the original John Deere. Hewitt set about turning the business into a multinational corporation, but without allowing it to lose its ethos.

Over his twenty-seven-year tenure, he subordinated his own personality to the rich heritage of the company. Hewitt loved to quote "past stories of conservative wisdom and leadership to fellow workers as a means of . . . reinforcing the values-based culture," according to David Magee's history of the company. Hewitt inspired trust in his employees as he helped Deere leapfrog past IH. When Hewitt retired, a colleague put it well: "He made us realize how good *we* were." It's hard to imagine higher praise for a leader—one who's capable of building trust among people and, just as important, empowering them to trust themselves.

It may sound like a paradox, but to be effective, high-trust leaders must see themselves as both vital and dispensable. Many leaders are indeed great men and women; the trick is not to announce it—and even more, not to believe it. When Julius Caesar rode in triumph into Rome to the roar of adoring crowds, he had a guard whisper repeatedly into his ear, "You are only a man." A leader's ego suspension is essential to learning from inevitable mistakes. Unless leaders have the modesty to learn, grow, and weather the journey along with everybody else, few will want to trust them.

Leaders might consider enthroning humility as a foundational element in trust building in these five ways:

1 **Remember the mantra: "It's about the mission, not about me."** You may be the leader, but don't confuse your identity with the organization's. Great people can create good organizations, but great organizations endure because of values that transcend any single individual.

2 **Gather the history of the organization.** This includes its founders, inventors, and remarkable contributors.

Choose the artwork you hang on the walls to capture the history of the firm and those who've worked there.

3 **Celebrate achievements openly—give recognition.** This is particularly important for the unseen heroes who toil in every organization to keep the trains running on time. Don't miss a chance to acknowledge and thank people. Gratitude is essential to trust.

4 **When thanking people, be specific.** Don't just say, "Thanks for the great job." Give details. And do it in front of their peers. For one thing, this will require leaders to do the work to know what went into the many things that are taken for granted every day in every organization.

5 **Look for fun, meaningful ways people can interact outside work.** Picnics, golf, ball games, and service projects are traditional activities many companies sponsor to build bonds within groups. JetBlue employees from every department have planted some four thousand trees in New York. And when Hurricane Sandy hit, crewmembers spent twenty-five thousand hours together delivering hot meals to those in distress. In the end, the crewmembers and New York City were all beneficiaries.

To BUILD A HIGH-TRUST enterprise, one needs to demonstrate personal integrity, invest in interpersonal respect, empower team members, measure what one wants to achieve, create a dream, communicate lavishly, and make conflict constructive. The Eighth Law of Trust is to have the self-insight, the self-skepticism—in short, the humility—to recognize the previous seven.

Building a durable, high-trust culture means focusing on the success and well-being of the organization as a whole, and primarily of individual team members who give it energy and life. If you want to be a high-trust leader, you've got to be in the center—without *being* the center.

• • •

KEY QUESTION

LAW 8: HUMILITY. My organization's leaders care more about doing what is right for its people, clients, and mission than they care about their own power and status.

1.	2.	3.	4.	5.
Strongly Disagree	Generally Disagree	Neutral	Generally Agree	Strongly Agree

STRIVE FOR WIN-WIN
NEGOTIATIONS

NATURALLY, IN NEGOTIATING WITH third parties, we must assess whether they can be trusted. We trust our lawyers to be fiduciaries for our interests in third-party negotiations, but there are lots of internal negotiations that are more like conversations—discussions where we're not represented by lawyers but where trust underpins the exchange. It's helpful to think of negotiations as conversations around trade-offs. Every conversation has a purpose. When your mindset is that you want the other party to "win"—to get something it wants too—you're on the road to successful negotiations. Whether being asked to pick up the kids or to come in under budget, people are constantly making trades with each other—in business, government, families, churches, and schools.

The stylized negotiations surrounding commercial transactions typically involve lawyers and accountants helping business leaders fuss over price, terms, time frames, remedies, and representations and warranties. Such negotiations can either build or destroy trust, as do the conversations that happen every day around the breakfast table or at the watercooler. Aware of the economy of trust—of the idea that today's conversation is one in a series, not a one-off—we tend to gracefully make trade-offs in the negotiations of daily life, adapting to the constant give-get that is a part of every high-trust relationship.

Contrast these everyday interactions with Hollywood's entertaining version of business negotiation, in which executives fight a verbal battle from either side of a long conference table, flanked by teams of lawyers, bankers, and consultants. Traps are set, voices are raised, and threats are made until one combatant maneuvers the others into a corner. Triumphantly, Gordon Gekko coldly declares himself the victor: "It's not a question of 'enough,' pal," he says. "It's a zero-sum game—somebody wins, somebody loses."

Thanks to such fictions, many people think the point of negotiation is to maximize immediate economic gain, without regard for the impact on the other side and without any sense that there are long-term consequences. A cottage industry has sprung up with self-styled negotiation experts offering ways to keep prospective employers, suppliers, and other "adversaries" on the ropes. But in the long run, treating negotiation as a boxing match will result in punches that should never have been thrown and a lot of unnecessary bloodshed.

A better way—one that builds rather than destroys trust—is described in the classic *Getting to Yes*, an early 1980s bestseller by Roger Fisher and William L. Ury, still taught in business schools. The book aims to show that when negotiators "separate the people from the problem," "focus on issues, not positions," and "invent options for mutual gain," they're more likely to find acceptable outcomes for all participants.[1]

In a sense, all negotiations are serial, not episodic, so imagine that you're slowly building a brand—a reputation that will follow you for your entire career. Extracting one killer deal from your counterpart can turn out to be costly in the long run. For one thing, you might forfeit the chance to do more business with the person or the people he or she is close to. For another, you may have done nothing more than create an unstable agreement.

Practicing and internalizing these six attitudes can help shape the way you build trust while sitting at the negotiating (or dinner) table:

1 **Assume this is but one conversation in an ongoing narrative.** Over the course of your career, you'll engage in thousands of negotiations. Getting your way at any cost is not the reputation you want. Though people may not remember the suboptimal result of a single exchange, they'll never forget how they felt when you dismissed their concerns or treated them disrespectfully. You're not obligated to make sure those on the other side get a great deal, but you do want them to walk away feeling respected. If they do, the opportunities that will come to you in the future will more than compensate for whatever it is you think you gave up to ensure a fair deal.

2 **Consider the other side's interests.** Understanding that your negotiating partners' interests are legitimate conveys respect. (Assume they may have anxieties about your trustworthiness too.) When they see your efforts to understand their perspective, they're likely to be more willing to engage in honest dialogue, which makes it easier to find a solution everyone sees as a win.

Think of your goal as putting a fair price on what the other parties want. It's up to them to decide if their demands are worth the price you've set. You'll know you're getting close when you can describe their needs in a way that satisfies them and they can acknowledge the price of what they're asking for.

3 **Aim to create value for all parties.** Nobody's counseling capitulation. The point isn't to pummel the other person into submission, as if you win only when he or she loses. If your counterpart benefits from doing business with you, and you walk away satisfied too, you've created two wins. Strengthening your relationship with the other party can mean more business, more referrals, a stronger brand, and more lasting agreements.

4 **Eschew psych-out tactics.** Many people start negotiations by assessing who has more legal or economic firepower, and who's more willing to walk away. This power-only mindset can negatively charge a discussion and get it off on the wrong foot, turning a contest of issues into a battle of wills.

You can avoid that by focusing first on the principles both sides agree on. Consider Lee Iacocca, the former CEO of Chrysler. His approach to negotiation was consistent with building trust in negotiations: "Being honest is the best technique I can use. Right up front, tell people what you're trying to accomplish and what you're willing to sacrifice to accomplish it."

5 **Find power in inquiry.** Most people will tell you what they want out of negotiations if you simply ask the right questions. In negotiation, as in life, doing more listening than talking is a good rule of thumb. Asking probing questions about the other party's perspective may yield insights into how to structure a deal. If the other side tells you its chief concern is price, and if you're willing to meet the price, you may be able to set the other terms. Understanding the interdependence of the five elements noted at the beginning of this chapter (price, terms, time frames, remedies, and representations and warranties) can help make for win-win agreements.

6 **Choose carefully the people you negotiate with.** It's tough to hold productive discussions with people who get no joy out of the process, and prefer Gekko fighting to finding creative solutions. As Trammell Crow used to tell me, "You can't do good business with bad people."

You can't come to fair agreements with people whose only concern is their own short-term gain, serving only their benighted self-interests. So if you're intent on building a high-trust organization, choose those who are already on the bus and thereby ensure that at least your internal negotiations are with people you trust. And follow George Bernard Shaw's advice: "Never wrestle with pigs. You both get dirty and the pig likes it." Try to negotiate (and hire and promote) only trustworthy people.

EACH CONVERSATION AND NEGOTIATION either advances or destroys trust. Building a brand for fairness deepens trust among all members of the team, resulting in flexible arrangements along with enjoyable relationships among teammates.

· · ·

KEY QUESTION

LAW 9: NEGOTIATIONS. Negotiations at my organization—whether between colleagues or with third parties—*rarely* leave people feeling taken advantage of.

1.	2.	3.	4.	5.
Strongly Disagree	Generally Disagree	Neutral	Generally Agree	Strongly Agree

FIX BREACHES IMMEDIATELY

ALL THREE KINDS OF relationships to which we apply the word *trust* can result in betrayal. Reciprocal trust can end in divorce or the breakup of an interdependent partnership. Representative trust can suffer breaches of fiduciary duty in which a trusted professional takes advantage of superior knowledge or training. And by the nature of pseudo trust, betrayal lies in wait when circumstances change, rendering it only a convenient substitute for real trust.

So there are ample reasons to be aware of the pitfalls of trust. But if one grants trust only after carefully evaluating character, competence, and authority, betrayal is less likely. This evaluation results in knowing whom to trust—or, stated differently, trust that's smart.

In difficult times, trust is a leader's most valuable currency. When we work alongside a leader whose integrity and vision we believe in and who, in turn, respects those around him or her—that's when the separation between high- and low-trust leaders is starkest.

Instead of reliance on the laws of trust, low-trust leaders must fall back on the use of raw power in time of crisis. When you work under such people, you'll soon see the telltale signs of low-trust leaders as they spend their energy manipulating the levers of power. Niccolò Machiavelli famously wrote, "It is much more secure to be feared than to be loved." That approach works—until it doesn't. Machiavelli wouldn't have been running a company of knowledge workers very successfully for very long.

When a CEO can't reverse a firm's cratering stock price, or when approval ratings for a member of Congress flatline, the power they used to get things done doesn't seem so potent anymore. Since they never cared enough (or paid the price) to create genuine trust among those with whom they work, when things go bad they discover they have nothing left to offer— and no one left to lead.

Indeed, in turnarounds and crises, the best asset any leader has is character—inspiring people to take leaps of faith with him or her. The best leaders work to build trust over the long term by thoughtfully and cautiously empowering others consistent with the 10 Laws of Trust. Leaders determined to build cultures in which trust is more than just a feel-good notion know it's hard work. "Earning trust is not easy, nor is it cheap, nor does it happen quickly," wrote Max De Pree, in *Leading Without Power: Finding Hope in Serving Community.*

"Trust comes only with genuine effort, never with a lick and a promise."[1]

It is not only organizations that are damaged in crises; careers are destroyed, and people fall short of their own potential. Leaders who think that by the exercise of dominion over others they are maximizing their own success find that no one follows them when they're without the tools of fear and reward. Perhaps worst of all, they miss the opportunity to develop lasting relationships, build enduring organizations, and create opportunities for growth and meaning, even as they fail to enjoy the satisfaction and peace that flow from being trusted—and trustworthy.

So, fully aware of the downsides of betrayal, one can successfully embrace the 10 Laws of Trust in order to build a lasting, effective organization. The trick is to do so with care. When figuring out whom to trust and under what circumstances, here are five mindsets to consider:

1 **In the moments of calm before crises, imagine yourself as duty-bound to lead.** The firefighters who entered the World Trade Center on September 11 had already made the decision to lead long before the crisis was upon them. They were bound to a decision they didn't have to make in the moment. Trustworthy leaders likewise are committed to lead when the chips are down. If trust has been nurtured, the commitment of team members will be reciprocated. Having worked through a few turnarounds, I can say that they're not

fun; I can also say that the bonds of trust forged in foxholes are unusually durable.

2 **Think of yourself as a fiduciary.** This means being a guardian of others' interests. Having a duty to others makes it more compelling to take on the hard tasks you might be reluctant to do if it were only about you. Indeed, living life by looking through a fiduciary lens is the best way to secure relationships rooted in trust.

3 **Expect that you'll have to keep running toward fires.** It takes time to build trust at a level that inspires people to run to the fires (see Law 7). There are no shortcuts. And if you're not careful, everything you've built can be forfeited in a minute. If you choose to lead by investing in trust, expect that you'll have to keep earning it by the consistent application of the laws of trust. The payoff—binding people together in powerful ways—will be worth it.

4 **Be mindful of the long term.** When tensions inexorably surface in your organization, take a break. Pick things up later. But be specific, so no one is left hanging: "Let's revisit this again tomorrow after we've all had time to think about it." That means tomorrow, not some indeterminate future.

5 **Fear not.** Rushing headlong into a management blaze can mean you miscalculate. Hold back too long and the chance to resolve the conflict and to learn from it vanishes. Choosing the moment takes judgment. Diffidence and doubt are not features of high-trust organizations. If you're faint-hearted, consider that fear is the tear in the trust fabric that creates the greatest risks during moments of truth. Since the deferral of problems usually means dealing with a bigger problem in an even less certain future, figure out why you're reluctant to run toward the fire and address it openly. Then focus on action. Despite my admonition to proceed with care, don't confuse caution with timidity.

HONORING THESE PRINCIPLES CAN make all the difference— to productivity, innovation, retaining knowledge workers and above all one's own happiness. But creating the bonds of trust that increase cooperation takes a lifelong commitment. If you embark on this journey and prudently observe its principles, you can be confident that the view will be worth the climb.

• • •

KEY QUESTION

LAW 10: BREACHES. In our most trying or critical situations, I trust our leaders to make decisions that are in the organization's best interests, including responding promptly and fairly with any breaches of trust.

1.	2.	3.	4.	5.
Strongly Disagree	Generally Disagree	Neutral	Generally Agree	Strongly Agree

HOW TO RESTORE TRUST

"Treachery and violence are spears pointed at both ends; they wound those who resort to them worse than their enemies."

—EMILY BRONTË, *WUTHERING HEIGHTS*

WE LABEL VIOLATIONS OF trust "betrayal." The natural fear of betrayal, taken to excess, greatly increases the difficulty of building a high-trust culture. Unfortunately, from the Bible to Shakespeare, from Benedict Arnold to Bernie Madoff, the double-cross is alive and well in every culture, during every era, and across every socioeconomic class.

Treachery may make for great literature or tragic history; but at ground level, it cripples organizations and destroys lives. And it is common enough that every person and organization needs to know not only how to avoid betrayal in the first place, but also how to overcome the devastation it causes.

The roots of betrayal—power, money, and pride—are as predictive of tragedy as the 10 Laws of Trust are requisite for building high-trust cultures. The negative emotions that flow from betrayal are toxic to any system and include depression, anger, and an unwillingness to take future leaps of faith.

Applying the 10 Laws of Trust to consciously build a high-trust organization is far more effective than constantly recovering from breaches of trust. But even in the best cultures, the latter may be occasionally necessary. As stumbles occur, knowing how to overcome them is vital to securing a high-trust culture.

In my own life, while investments in trust have led to stability, lifelong friendships, and a series of mostly profitable business ventures, overcoming the abiding danger of a breach and regaining my footing after a betrayal have been nearly as valuable.

Initially, betrayal breaks the heart of the victim. It invades the spirit, becoming an inchoate reminder—with an exasperatingly long half-life—that something is wrong. Unless victims overcome the toxic effects of the offense, they risk denying themselves a fully productive and happy life.

Betrayal—though devastating at its instant of discovery—need not signal the end of one's ability to trust. Indeed, betrayal teaches one to trust based on an increasingly critical assessment of the (1) character, (2) competence, and (3) authority of those to whom one considers granting trust. Indeed, to trust in the absence of all three of these underpinnings is to expose oneself to those who are (1) insecure, (2) hypercompetitive, or (3) fundamentally dissatisfied with their own lives.

These are harbingers. Placing trust in somebody who suffers from any of the following three unmet needs is risky: (1) a desperate need for security, (2) a need to win at all costs, or (3) a general malaise. All three can presage responses that one would never suspect in people who might otherwise be trustworthy. By being alert to such insidious internal wiring, one can decide who is safe to hire, to do business with, or even to marry.

As with most clouds, there is a silver lining. For me, betrayal became an unwanted and unexpected gift. From betrayal, I've learned to harvest four otherwise hard-to-come-by benefits:

1. Escaping one-sided relationships.
2. Developing the grit to rebound.
3. More fully appreciating those who are trustworthy.
4. Better assessing at the outset those likely to disappoint.

Without having suffered betrayal, I'd still be stuck in an unsatisfying dead-end partnership, hesitant to take on new challenges, and undervaluing my truest friends. For me, the soul-crushing costs of betrayal triggered a ruthless trimming of the false, the superficial, and the transitory, anchoring me to a bedrock from which I might begin anew.

The first time you're betrayed, you can't imagine having been used by someone you trusted. At first, you hope it isn't so. Then you try to understand why and how you were duped. Finally, you accept—if you're honest with yourself—that *you* helped create the circumstances that led to the betrayal. Most betrayals are "joint-ventured," either by a failure to trust wisely in the first place, or by a willful blindness to something that is not right. While hard to accept, most of us play starring roles in our own betrayal.

When I first discovered I'd been part of a betrayal, I felt isolated, until I realized that virtually *everyone* suffers the occasional betrayal at another's hands—or worse, betrays someone else. If only because unresolved betrayal limits one's willingness to hazard trust, healing is vital.

To commit to healing fully, you will eventually have to offer the unnatural act of forgiving the party who betrayed you—as well as forgiving yourself. You do not have to rebuild the relationship that let you down; you merely have to let go. Only then will you have a shot at full recovery. Above all, this is a decision to prioritize the future over the past. It will take time to come to this conclusion. It will take the vision of a brighter future if you are to let go of a darker but more familiar past. Like Cortés's order to burn the ships at Veracruz, you must no longer allow yourself the possibility of falling back on the familiar past if you are to embrace the uncertain future.

But this is easier said than done.

Learning to (1) compromise and (2) overcome failure are the two most vital and difficult learned skills for any leader. Appendix B offers two real-life but disguised accounts of betrayal in the form of business-school cases, followed by discussion questions that may be used by interdependent teams to discuss how to overcome what Shakespeare called the "*most unkindest cut of all.*"

• • •

HIGH-TRUST GROUPS DON'T HAPPEN by accident, and they don't happen overnight. They're created painstakingly, by leaders disciplined in their exercise of the 10 Laws of Trust. Molière was correct: "Trees that are slow to grow bear the best fruit." Taking all of the conscious steps to build a high-trust culture is a patient, one-person-at-a-time, one-conversation-at-a-time process.

And it's worth it. Negotiating with, raising children with, and building businesses with trustworthy people makes life rewarding. Reinforced by good experiences, our bias is to trust—to act as if betrayal is unlikely. This turns out to be a pretty good bet if the decision to grant trust is grounded firmly in the three core conditions for trust introduced in the previous chapter: character, competence, and the authority to deliver. And if, after having chosen to trust those who meet these tests, we secure that trust by following the 10 Laws for building high-trust relationships, the odds of betrayal diminish dramatically.

Of course, there will always be those who betray trust. The offenders tend to see life only through their own eyes, ever disconnected and self-referencing. They're blind to the linkage of events and relationships that becomes obvious when seeing life through a wide-angle lens. Positioning themselves at the center of their own universe condemns betrayers to seeing others as tools—mere enablers or obstacles to immediate objectives. In each of its forms, trust for them is subject to breach. Its apparent existence may even be used as a lure and a weapon.

The reassuring news remains that most professionals do in fact honor the trust granted by clients. Indeed, when it comes to representative or reciprocal trust, my own experience is that virtually all paid fiduciaries are trustworthy and faithful stewards on whom one can rely—in part because the downside of being untrustworthy is so high. And the vast majority of people honor their partners' interests as their own.

Even so, nobody is invariably reliable or everlastingly trustworthy, be it for reasons of character, competence, or lack of authority. Thus, one must go into trust relationships understanding what to do in the event of betrayal. A small fraction of those you think you can trust are con artists—proficient not at the tasks you hired them for, but at justification, cover-up, and pretense. Others are inept or inadequately empowered to deliver on their promises. Even the good-hearted and capable may fail to deliver at a moment of crisis, whether under the weight of external factors or bad judgment or simply a lack of authority. We should all expect a breakdown in trust somewhere in our future. He who seems at first blush to be Warren Buffett may in reality be Bernie Madoff.

Because there are no guarantees, we need to know what to do if our trust turns out to have been ill-placed after all. As indispensable as trust is as a catalyst for innovation, decision making, and the durability of contracts, it can fail us. That said, the wariest among us, setting up elaborate policing mechanisms, risk a different kind of failure—of missed opportunity, of life never animated by the collaborative energy that comes from trust wisely granted.

The 10 Laws of Trust, if not followed or if implemented with scoundrels, are no guarantee against the risk of betrayal. But in the end, the odds of betrayal can be minimized, and its damage to one's psyche overcome, if one understands seven realities:

1 **Betrayal at some point is likely.** Early in my real estate development career, I learned something about being insufficiently vigilant. Frank (not his real name) seemed a capable young associate. He enthusiastically recommended moving forward with a significant real estate project. At the same time, he secretly wrote his own confidential memo "to the file," summarizing the project's downside and recommending against doing the very project he'd just advised me to take on. Frank figured he had devised a shrewd plan to cover his bases no matter what happened. Based on his persuasive oral presentation (and obviously not on what he had opined in writing), I moved forward with the project. As it turned into a smashing success, my trust in Frank grew; my firm made him a partner and expanded his responsibilities.

Had I read Frank's incongruous secret memo, I would have quickly reckoned that my trust had been misplaced and that Frank was not worthy of trust, much less a promotion. Trustworthy people don't act as he did. Only Frank knew about both versions of the analysis he'd done. His slippery calculus turned on the reality that it would be more than four years before the results of the real estate project came in. If they were good, as expected, he'd rightfully point to being instrumental in pushing the project along. By contrast, if results were poor, he'd have a memo in the file outlining his reservations, and maybe that would come in handy.

Years later, an assistant uncovered Frank's contradictory memo, and I confronted Frank. His explanation was that he'd been raised in a culture that punished mistakes so severely that its members were reluctant ever to hazard a recommendation. When pressed, as he put it, "to put a stake in the ground," his nature was to hedge his bet, just in case punishment loomed. Because of that, Frank instinctively betrayed a trust that would be hard to restore.

When Frank's duplicity surfaced, one of my fellow partners commented, "Frank's genius was wasted inside a partnership. His real talent was spin, doublespeak, and cover-up." These might be considered "skills" in low-trust contexts, but in a partnership or in a marriage—requiring supreme trust, where transparency is the bedrock—they undermine its chief currency. It was impossible for me to fully trust Frank again without an effort on his part to restore trust. The breach of trust arising from his stealth memo, coupled with his failure to reconcile, made moving to a new career his next step.

2   **Betrayal stings.** Breaches of fiduciary duty feel worse than breaches of contract. When we're betrayed, we didn't

just have our car broken into or lose our mother's heirloom ring. We were duped by someone we trusted. We turned over our trust to them, and they violated it. Even worse, somewhere in the deep recesses of our consciousness, we fear that the betrayal was made possible by a suspension of caution on our part.

After Madoff was exposed in 2008 as the greatest Ponzi-scheme fraudster in American history, one money manager told me he'd been pressured by several of his investors to get them into Madoff's funds. They were in effect begging to be taken advantage of. After visiting Madoff's office in Midtown Manhattan early on in Madoff's run, my friend had remarked that Madoff could just be a guy with a printer and a creative accountant. As a result, to the chagrin of his well-heeled clients, my friend had declined to invest their capital with Bernie. Much later, his investors called to thank him for not having been taken in.

In businesses and partnerships, as in friendships and marriages, there's a natural tendency to accept things as they seem to be and as we want them to be. This is why con artists thrive—and why betrayal stings. Madoff's investors look back on what happened and wonder how they could possibly have been so gullible. Their expected response might be never to trust again.

3   **Betrayal isn't always personal.** Betrayal isn't limited to partners or fiduciaries, or to spouses or uncles. The public's trust can be breached. In one of the most notorious recent examples, cyclist Lance Armstrong finally admitted to

chronic blood doping in pursuit of his seven Tour de France titles. Capping the astonishing downfall of a once-revered athlete, Armstrong did so only after years of vehement public denial. Even then, he seemed to rationalize that his victories were legitimate because, supposedly, everybody else did it and he was therefore just leveling the playing field. The perverse message: If everybody betrays, nobody betrays. So when it comes to evaluating trust, along with appreciating the importance of caution, remember this corollary: After the breach of trust come the rationalizations. The betrayer rarely comes clean. He equivocates, he prevaricates, he quibbles. Tap dancing is his finest move; it might even impress you. You must then be doubly wary of the rationalization that follows the betrayal.

In Armstrong's case, the betrayal had been so well hidden that it took years to strip down the bulwarks built by those who had a vested interest in shielding him. And it doesn't take a cynic to realize that Armstrong's deception could have carried on for years more. But ultimately, his plunge was breathtaking and the wreckage colossal. The sports icon went from heroic cancer survivor to pariah. The public swiftly rejected Armstrong's narrative in spite of all the good he had done.

Just as President Richard Nixon lost his place in history by lying about a "third-rate burglary" and President Bill Clinton hurt his legacy by cavorting with "that intern," Armstrong forfeited his own good name. Most of the time, trust is one-way sticky. One can destroy in a minute a trust that took years to build, and it might never be fully recovered.

4 **Reconciliation is possible, if difficult.** Reconciliation means both parties squarely facing the breach of trust and agreeing to put it behind them. And of course, the betrayer must apologize to the damaged party. Neither Armstrong nor Madoff, nor, for that matter, my work colleague Frank, attempted to reconcile with those they had betrayed—perhaps so much the better. Ordinarily, it is a far better use of everyone's energy to invest in forming bonds with those willing to pay the price to follow the laws of trust. In some cases, the discovery of a violation is a merciful trigger that exposes what was counterfeit in the first place. Many marriages end this way. The same happens in business partnerships.

There are several steps to take if one's trust has been betrayed:

- **Accept some responsibility.** While the blame lies with the betrayer, rarely does the betrayed not play any role in being duped. As painful as this realization is, it can be the first step to recovery.
- **Recognize you're not alone.** Accept that others, no doubt, have also been duped.
- **Consider the seriousness of the breach.** While the routine required for building trust in the first place is akin to getting in shape one workout at a time, restoring trust will be more like recovering from a car accident in which the body has been shattered. As with the triage any emergency-room team must undertake

with each victim, any chance at restoration begins with a diagnosis of the severity of the damage.

In other words, whiplash is one thing, a severed spinal cord quite another. Just as the severely injured may have limited physical recovery options, so may relationships that have suffered certain breaches of trust. Getting a once-healthy relationship back to being functional may simply be a matter of clearing up misunderstandings. Or it may be that options are limited. If the latter is the diagnosis in a case of breached trust, we will ask if we ought to spend any time rebuilding it.

- **Fix quickly what can be fixed.** When a betrayal can be explained as a one-off stumble, perhaps born of extenuating circumstances, it may well be worth giving the betrayer another chance. There's plenty of room for redemption in these cases that will benefit both the forgiver and the forgiven. The other instance in which it may be worth fixing things is where the upside is great. In breaches of trust between partners in a marriage, especially when children are involved, it may pay to seek reconciliation simply because so much is at stake.

5 The steps toward restoration are demanding.

Restoration means restitution—paying for economic and psychological damage so the parties can begin anew. Just as there are principles for building trust in the first place, there are principles that govern restoring broken trust. While the odds of restoring trust to former levels are low—and even in cases when an ultimate restoration is unachievable—it helps to follow these rules:

- **Be realistic about the potential.** Start with no illusions: The process for restoring broken trust is different from building it. Recovering from betrayal is harder, more costly—and, worst of all, less likely to succeed—than securing trust at the outset. This clearly suggests that should there arise even a perceived breach of trust along the way to building a high-trust culture, it's smart to address it before it metastasizes. Once broken, trust is Humpty-Dumptyian—hard to put back together again.

- **Forgive.** Move on, unburdened by the weight of treachery. Forgiveness is key; even dime-store psychologists recognize that those who harbor bitterness damage themselves above all. Giving in to revenge is almost as if the betrayer takes a second, deeper cut out of us. We never get beyond the grievance; we ruminate to the point of distraction; we allow our own contentment to be measured by the amount of flesh we've extracted from an adversary. Even in betrayal, "love your enemies" works better than "an eye for an eye." Forgiveness becomes easier when one realizes it will have no effect on the forgiven party—other than perhaps to confuse the individual. But forgiveness can give us our own life back.

- **Don't consider trying to get even.** Vengeance is rarely sweet. The downside of retribution is that it leads to self-absorption. A far more productive process is engaging in mourning the loss—after which there's an opportunity to think through what happened and to try to correct flaws, be they structural (bad hiring, bad oversight), or personal (your own inattention to trust's fundamental requirement for character, competence, and authority), or laziness (including just plain naïveté).

    Years ago, I felt betrayed by someone whom I was certain I could never forgive. A good friend gave me a copy of *The Count of Monte Cristo* so that I could vicariously live what I thought I most wanted. Over a weekend, I devoured Alexandre Dumas's classic novel, enjoying the payback designed by Edmond Dantès. But as subtext, I realized that Dantès's deliciously complex scheme resulted not only in destroying the three men who had shattered his life, but also in taking him to the brink of his own destruction, depriving him of joy, hollowing him out along with the deserving objects of his contempt. He had "become them"—winning a battle but losing the war.

- **If restoration is possible, construct it carefully.** In a few instances, forgiveness may plow a pathway to trust's restoration. The three crucial preconditions are:

1. A genuine recognition on the part of the betrayer of the breach and of the damage caused from the perspective of the betrayed.
2. An earnest apology that acknowledges the violation of trust (without rationalizations or "buts")—preferably sooner rather than later—and that takes responsibility instead of blaming external factors. As one young entrepreneur once taught me, "You've not apologized until the other party accepts your apology." Restoring trust is a two-way process.
3. A willingness to fix things—to make restitution.

- **Accept the apology.** There's no exact formula for adequate remorse. A person's apology may sound sincere, yet only be another con by a practiced scoundrel. Some people make their living as con artists, creating "trust me" moments. I once worked with an individual who continually proclaimed that he "always put my interests ahead of his." Looking back on it, he claimed virtue too often. (Hamlet's mom was right: you *can* protest too much.) Predictably, my former colleague never apologized, sought reconciliation, or came close to the idea of restitution. My only option was to forgive and move on. I could tell I'd forgiven when my focus turned to the future.

At the end of the day, all you can do is use your best judgment in gauging another's attempt to make amends. You'll probably know contrition when you see it. If you make the call that the relationship is worth resuming, then embrace it and focus on the future. In the case of one betrayal that affected me, after choosing to forgive, I determined to correct the deficiencies in my own analysis of trust that cost me so dearly. I then closed the chapter by deciding never again to do business with the self-centered, the defensive, or the remorseless.

6   **Institutions and companies betray—and can recover too.** On occasion, companies facing crises that are defined by a breach of trust emerge stronger as a result. Consider JetBlue. In February 2007, an ice storm pummeled the East Coast, resulting in widespread aviation delays and cancellations. As the largest carrier out of John F. Kennedy International Airport in New York City, where all takeoffs had been halted, JetBlue was hit hardest. The airline's communications and reservations technology didn't allow it to deal adequately with passengers stranded in the terminal and on runways. Many other airlines suffered as well during what became known as the "Valentine's Day Massacre."

JetBlue's response was aggressive and apologetic at the same time. Founder and CEO David Neeleman took to all the TV networks to own up. In a voice a reporter described as "cracking," Neeleman told the *New York Times* he was "humiliated and mortified." And well before Congress took action against the entire industry, JetBlue quickly issued a Customer Bill of Rights, offering compensation for overbooking and a range of delays. It cost the company a lot of money, and, as chairman, I initially told Neeleman he might have been too remorseful and apologetic. After all, we had an excellent reputation and had built up much goodwill with consumers. Could we not just have apologized without making specific financial concessions? As it turned out, Neeleman was right and I was wrong. We recovered from the debacle, in part because our apology was not only sincere, but also included voluntary efforts at restitution.

You can think of relationships—in the marketplace and in your personal life—as a set of deposits and withdrawals. At JetBlue, devotion over the years to being people-friendly was a major deposit. The Valentine's Day Massacre was a big withdrawal. Expressing a genuine apology, offering compensation, and creating the Customer Bill of Rights were new deposits that helped the company recoup public confidence.

7 **Trust is worth the risk.** In all human relationships, the virtue of trust is undeniable. But it is not without peril. People are human; temptations abound; trust can take a beating. Trusting others carries a contingent price. However, not trusting others carries an even higher current price. The bonds created in high-trust relationships are the ones that give life

meaning. If you're too wary, too worried, you'll wind up with fewer opportunities and fewer human connections. You'll spend your life calculating, protecting yourself, expecting the worst, and trying to secure the power and position that will serve what you think will bring you happiness, wealth, or fame. Instead, you'll either live a stunted life, or you will condemn those who work with you to smaller lives than they deserve.

Over the course of more than four decades in business, in the context of more than twenty-three hundred different investments—involving startups, turnarounds, and rapid-growth companies—I've worked with hundreds of investors and partners all over the world, and thousands of employees in companies across multiple industries. And I've taught thousands of young people destined to be tomorrow's leaders. I'm delighted to report that the mindset of Frank, my former partner, has been rare.

Almost all my partners and virtually all the paid professionals I've retained have taken their obligations seriously. In my experience, the small set of exceptions stand out as object lessons among otherwise high-trust relationships. Having been betrayed, I still opt for trust over mistrust, reliance over flying solo, and applying the 10 Laws of Trust over the protections of the paranoid. Now, however, I take more care to be certain that character, competence, and authority are all present in every trust relationship. I pay more careful attention to my choice of partners and representatives, and to the need for accountability.

After many years in business, in a family, in a community—in short, in living a fortunate life—I've concluded that carefully managed trust is well worth the risk. Indeed, living life without deeply trusting others is even riskier, a whole lot less satisfying, and much less likely to result in maximizing potential. To all who must necessarily trust in order to lead and be led by others, I offer my life experience as proof of the extraordinary power of trust and the ennobling adventure of working in high-trust environments.

A DIAGNOSTIC TOOL

DETERMINING YOUR ORGANIZATION'S TRUST level is vital to increasing it. However, because of the emotional nature of trust, many people are reluctant to talk about their wariness, misgivings, and fears of betrayal.

Training leader FranklinCovey has developed a tool based on *The 10 Laws of Trust*. The diagnostic tool that follows has been tested statistically and psychometrically to give leaders a starting point for addressing their current state of organizational trust in order to build the interdependencies upon which high-trust relationships depend.

For a confidential organizational scoring of this evaluation of organizational-trust levels, go to www.10lawsoftrust.com.

•   •   •

· WHAT IS THE TRUST LEVEL OF MY ORGANIZATION? ·

Ask each team member to respond to the following ten statements about the organization using a scale of 1 to 5:

1.	2.	3.	4.	5.
Strongly Disagree	Generally Disagree	Neutral	Generally Agree	Strongly Agree

· TESTING EACH LAW ·

- **Law 1: Integrity.** Leaders in my organization *consistently* align their behaviors with the principles to which they aspire.
- **Law 2: Respect.** Individuals in my organization behave respectfully *to a much greater extent* than they behave disrespectfully in their dealings with each other and with customers, suppliers, or other third parties.
- **Law 3: Empowerment.** My organization encourages me to be innovative and to take calculated risks without fearing unfair shame or punishment.
- **Law 4: Measures.** I trust the processes by which my work is evaluated.
- **Law 5: Vision.** When I think of the most important thing my organization aims to do, I feel a sense of pride.
- **Law 6: Communication.** In my organization I usually have the information I need to do my job—and

when I don't, I know I can get it without being dismissed or patronized.

- **Law 7: Conflict.** I can point to instances where the *best* ideas won—even though they weren't popular or endorsed by my organization's loudest or most prominent leaders.
- **Law 8: Humility.** My organization's leaders care more about doing what is right for its people, clients, and mission than they care about their own power and status.
- **Law 9: Negotiations.** Negotiations at my organization—whether between colleagues or with third parties—*rarely* leave people feeling taken advantage of.
- **Law 10: Breaches.** In our most trying or critical situations, I trust our leaders to make decisions that are in the organization's best interests, including responding promptly and fairly to any breaches of trust.

· ORGANIZATIONAL TRUST SCORECARD ·

Tallying the individual ratings will yield an assessment score of between 10 and 50:

< 25	26–35	26–45	46+
Below Average	Average	Above Average	Exceptional

TWO CASES OF BETRAYAL

[WITH DISCUSSION QUESTIONS]

B OTH CASES ARE WORKS of fiction provided solely for illustrative purposes as a teaching device. All names, characters, and locations are fictitious. No identification with actual persons (living or deceased) should be inferred. Any resemblance to actual events, locales, or persons, living or dead, is coincidental.

CASE 1: A SHOWDOWN: MAIN STREET VS. WALL STREET

"Greed is a bottomless pit which exhausts the person
in an endless effort to satisfy the need without
ever reaching satisfaction."

—ERIC FROMM

In December 2011, Alexandra ("Alex") Brennan (not her real name), managing partner of AB Partners, a fictional West Coast private-equity firm, caught a red-eye from LAX to JFK. She had scheduled two brief days of meetings, planning to then head home to enjoy the holidays with her family. A week later, however, still in NYC, she flipped on her television to see protesters only blocks from her Lower Manhattan hotel. Alex would soon have sympathy for the "Occupy Wall Street" movement, as she found herself caught in the Venus flytrap of one of Wall Street's most fearsome banks.

Hanalei Technologies (HanaTech), an enterprise software company in which AB Partners held a 9½ percent stake, had fallen under the influence of a large investment bank (the "Bank"). The Bank had failed to refinance $700 million of HanaTech's (the "Company's") debt, carrying an extremely high 15 percent coupon. This was debt the Bank had arranged in prior years and for which it was now the syndicate manager. The Bank blamed refinancing delays on "debt markets roiled by the European debt crisis." Alex was not surprised by the year-end delay; but she was bewildered by the proposed bridge financing.

In the days that followed, the Bank's multiple relationships with the Company would force the Company to the brink of insolvency in a gambit that to Alex looked every bit like the shakedown of a Main Street firm.

* * *

· THE HOOK ·

The week prior to Alex's trip, the Bank—which also held a 24 percent ownership stake in HanaTech—had offered a "take it or pay the consequences" proposal to provide HanaTech with a $50 million bridge loan. According to the Bank, the new loan would need to be in place by the week before Christmas because of the specter of a technical default and bankers' vacation plans. For the holiday bridge loan, the Bank stood to receive a rate of return of more than 100 percent.

Alex had suggested that HanaTech simply raise the $50 million from its existing shareholders in the form of equity capital. HanaTech's core business had been performing well. And its investors were well-heeled. To her surprise, the Bank informed Alex that it had given an existing loan syndicate member (1) "blocking rights" on bringing any new equity capital into the Company, along with (2) a right to participate in 30 percent of any bridge financing. Furthermore, as the manager of the syndicate of lenders, the Bank had written into loan documents that it had a right to issue and take down the other 70 percent of any bridge loan. When the Bank failed in its agency assignment to refinance the Company's debt, it had fallen back on provisions it had written into loan documents.

When shareholders representing the other 76 percent of the ownership voiced objections (due to the loan's high cost and resulting economic dilution), the Bank responded that it might consider allocating up to 10 percent of the bridge loan to the other shareholders. However, the Bank now threatened that if other board-member shareholders failed to approve the terms of the bridge loan, the Bank would pounce from its perch as lender, put HanaTech into default, and seize control of the business.

To Alex, the threat was breathtaking. After all, the Bank was (1) a lender to HanaTech, (2) the manager of its debt syndicate, (3) a 24 percent shareholder (via its investments group), and (4) a member of HanaTech's board of directors. In two decades of service on various boards, Alex had never witnessed anything like the Bank's multiple control levers. In addition, she was stunned that HanaTech's reason for seeking new financing had been that it was groaning under 15 percent interest rates—the rate the Bank had arranged for the entirety of the Company's debt. The Bank's failure to refinance the Company's overpriced debt had created a moment of acute vulnerability for HanaTech. To Alex, it seemed that the Bank had manufactured the crisis for its own gain—a conflict of interest of the most treacherous kind.

Struggling to make sense of it, Alex learned that if HanaTech's board didn't accept the Bank's terms, the Bank would call the debt and foreclose on contracts put up as collateral and worth 150–175 percent of the outstanding debt. Although the lenders would easily be repaid in an orderly sale of the contracts, the Bank pointed out that "under the hammer," their value would be heavily discounted, putting shareholders at risk. And though the Bank was a shareholder, its net economic interest could be greatly enhanced from its perch as a debt holder.

HanaTech's worried executive team ("Management") had built an exceptional business that had garnered unsolicited offers to buy HanaTech at more than two times the value of its outstanding debt. Thus, in Alex's view, the debt was fully secured, and the creditors' risk of loss minimal.

To further sharpen its holiday ultimatum, the Bank reminded HanaTech of the debt covenants that allowed no time to cure any default, be it a cash-flow shortfall or a technical default as minor as a reporting delay. To demonstrate its resolve, the Bank announced that it had started monitoring currency exchange rates on a continuous basis because loan covenants were tied to the exchange rate between the US and Australian dollar. If rates moved in favor of the Australian dollar—even for a single second—the Bank threatened Management that the lenders could take over HanaTech, halt its operations, and liquidate its assets. Panicked, Management pleaded with the other shareholders to accept the Bank's Christmas demands.

Alex was especially unnerved by statements from the young associate the Bank had assigned to serve on HanaTech's board. Unmoved by shareholder objections, the associate threatened that the Bank's offer was what he called "take it or lose it" financing, bristling, "If you can bring $50 million to the table by Friday, the board will consider it; otherwise, the Bank's deal is the only one on the table."

With the clock ticking, Alex contacted the Bank's CEO to secure a meeting with the associate's boss, a senior Bank officer (the "Director").

· THE FIRST MEETING ·

Alex reached the Bank's CEO on Sunday afternoon to set up a 4:30 p.m. meeting the next day with the Director of the investments group supervising the relationship with HanaTech. The investments group was known both outside and inside the Bank as its shrewdest, most profitable unit.

Alex arrived thirty minutes early, eager to meet the person in charge of the Bank's relationship with HanaTech. She had three objectives:

1. To understand the Bank's proposal—was there a chance her concerns might be based on insufficient information?
2. To encourage the Bank to invite all shareholders to participate pro rata in any new financing—might there be a more equitable solution to HanaTech's needs?
3. To inform the Bank that she could not allow her Fund investors to be diluted by the nonmarket terms of the Bank's proposed bridge financing, when they were fully capable of funding the $50 million transaction themselves.

Alex planned to wait in the reception area. But there was no such area. The doors were all locked. And there was no indication that the offices were even part of the Bank.

After standing in the empty elevator lobby for several minutes, she hailed a young man, revealing to him whom she had come to see. He ushered her through an unmarked door into a vast landscaped office filled with desks at which young associates were seated shoulder to shoulder gazing into banks of glowing screens. He parked Alex in a conference room, and the Director arrived five minutes later.

After exchanging pleasantries, Alex asked how the interest rate on HanaTech's outstanding $700 million debt had ended up at 15 percent, roughly double the market rate. The Director replied: "Each time a new lender comes into our syndicate, the interest rate on the entire $700 million is ratcheted up to the rate required to cover the risk on the last dollar borrowed."

Incredulous, Alex asked: "How does that make any sense? Why wouldn't one simply create tranches of debt and price them according to the coverage provided by the underlying security?" (Typically, the more senior and less risky the security, the lower the return required by investors.) Only the last, least-secure dollar could conceivably have been priced at an interest rate approaching the 15 percent rate on the entire loan. The Director nodded: "It didn't make any sense to me, either; but this is what the Company agreed to."

Alex moved on to the next matter: "How about a rights offering to raise $50 million of equity from all existing shareholders on a pro rata basis?" Applying a non-dilutive formula for raising capital seemed to Alex the right way to protect all shareholders.

The Director's response was terse: "We need to be paid."

Alex responded: "The Bank will be paid—and handsomely—in a rights offering that treats all shareholders the same."

With its 24 percent stake as a shareholder, the Bank would receive nearly a quarter of any rights offering, in addition to a pro rata share of whatever the other shareholders declined to purchase. And since Management had already indicated it didn't have liquidity, the unsubscribed amounts related to its 40 percent ownership would be significant and would be allocated pro rata among the other shareholders, including the Bank.

Alex calculated aloud: "The Bank should end up with roughly $25 million of the $50 million offering. And at that participation level, it should make an extra $20 million profit in six months on a $25 million investment."

The Director shot back, "That's not enough."

In all of Alex's years of board service, she'd never known a board member to engineer what is known as a "cramdown" of other shareholders. She asked, "How can the Bank propose this, given the board's fiduciary duty to protect all shareholders?"

Before she could complete her question, the Director interjected: "We're not on the board."

"How could this be?" Alex wondered. The prior October all board members had signed a formal resolution to appoint a

Bank representative to the board. Furthermore, each board member had signed documents to appoint the young associate as the Bank's representative. And HanaTech's counsel had even sent confidential board materials to the Bank, who then joined the other Directors in appointing itself as agent to arrange the delayed refinancing that had triggered the Bank's ultimatum.

The Director informed Alex matter-of-factly that the Bank had never returned the document signed by all other board members to admit its young associate to the board. As a result, technically, the Bank was not on the board and was exempt from the legal standard of fiduciary duty owed by board members to shareholders.

This would make Gordon Gekko blush, Alex thought to herself. Was HanaTech the Bank's client, a counterparty, an investment—or all three?

Alex made a plea to the Director's sense of fairness: "What if we agreed that, since we [AB Partners] and the Bank are each capable of providing the capital for any bridge financing, our relative ownership percentages remain the same before and after the new issuance?"

Making sure he understood Alex's proposal, the Director responded: "So are you suggesting that if the ratio of the Bank's to AB Partners' net economics is now 80/20, that it remain the same after the offering?"

"Exactly," Alex replied, knowing this would produce a rights offering that would protect every shareholder. Alex then moved to her final point—alerting the Bank that under no circumstances would she permit her Fund's investors to wonder why they weren't invited to fund a pro rata share of the extremely expensive new financing. She summarized: "Even if [the Bank] has decided that it possesses no fiduciary duty to HanaTech's shareholders, I have a clear duty as a general partner to protect my limited partners' ["LPs'"] interests."

The Director demurred, promising to get back to Alex by the following morning. Sure enough, the next morning, Alex awoke to an email from the Director that read:

> "We are currently working with the intention of allowing AB Partners to invest their pro rata amount (9.5% of the $50mm bridge-loan issuance), in accordance with the preemptive rights afforded by the shareholder agreement (i.e., the $4.7 million that would protect them from dilution)."

Alex had achieved the objective of protecting her investors. However, she was disappointed that the Bank had rejected inviting all shareholders to participate pro rata.

· FOLLOW-UP ·

On the way to JFK, Alex received an urgent call on her cell phone from the CEO of HanaTech. In the back seat of a cab bouncing along Queens Boulevard, Alex sat stunned as the CEO accused her of interfering by calling on the Bank.

Alex explained, "I merely offered to take up to $10 million so they—or we—could offer all shareholders a chance to participate in the bridge loan."

The CEO responded:

"You don't understand. The Bank will blow up HanaTech if it doesn't get what it wants! By calling on the Bank directly, you got other shareholders mad, thinking they're not getting a fair share of the bridge loan. I even had to tell a cofounder that he cannot sign up for ANY of this financing, just to keep the Bank happy. If you don't limit your interest to the $4.7 million the Bank has offered your investors to protect them from dilution, you'll tank HanaTech."

Clearly, the Bank had relayed to the CEO that it had agreed to protect AB Partners from dilution by offering it a pro rata participation in the expensive bridge financing. Troubled by the CEO's distress, Alex responded, "Doesn't this tell you all you need to know about the predatory nature of this financing?"

Instead of examining her analysis, the stressed-out CEO responded: "I'm begging you not to blow up HanaTech. I'll have to fire thousands of people on Monday unless you agree to limit your participation in the bridge loan to $4.7 million."

Alex assured him that she had no interest in damaging HanaTech and would gladly accept the minimum investment allocation needed to protect her LPs. She also told him that she would rely on the board to do its duty to ensure every shareholder was given the same opportunity—a less-than-subtle reminder to the CEO of his own duty of care and loyalty to shareholders.

As soon as Alex landed in Los Angeles, she put her team to work. First, they prepared an alternative term sheet to the Bank's bridge financing, not only providing the board with more reasonable financing terms, but making participation in the financing available pro rata to all shareholders. Next, she and her team held an emergency Investment Committee meeting to arrange for up to $50 million of funding to be made available to support AB Partners' more attractive term sheet.

While preparing materials for her Investment Committee, Alex received an email from HanaTech's CEO marked: "Urgent Matter!" The CEO noted that the Bank had completed its allocation for existing shareholders and had agreed to increase from the 10 percent it presented in the face-to-face meeting in New York. Now it would allow those who owned 76 percent of HanaTech to participate in up to 17 percent ($8.5 million) of the $50 million bridge loan. Alex responded that she hoped this would satisfy any demand by other shareholders; and if it represented more than enough to satisfy demand from other shareholders, she wondered if it might represent a further pro rata opportunity for the AB Fund.

Knowing her Investment Committee's attitude, Alex said, "We're prepared to take the whole $8.5 million, go as low as

$4.7 million—simply to protect our LPs—or do anything in between." With this, Alex also informed the CEO that AB Partners would formally submit to the board an alternative term sheet to fund the entire $50 million bridge loan, giving Management an option.

Alex received no response from the CEO or the Bank.

· THE STING ·

Friday was the date of the board meeting at which HanaTech and Management would decide which bridge loan proposal to accept—the Bank's, or the cheaper one from AB Partners. As the deadline approached, Alex called the board to ask if she should be wiring money. To her surprise and disappointment, the board informed her that it had selected the Bank's more expensive term sheet. To her dismay, the Bank had also unilaterally reduced the allocation to AB Partners from the promised $4.7 million allocation to only $2 million.

The CEO asserted that "certainty of funding" had been the overriding factor in its decision. Furthermore, the CEO went on, the board had determined that AB Partners' approval wasn't required for the transaction, hence the sudden unilateral "haircut."

Alex stepped outside for some fresh air. It would be a long weekend.

· · ·

· TIME FOR HARDBALL ·

With little time left, Alex possessed but two options: accept the $2 million participation now offered, or fight for her LPs' interests as shareholders. With less than half of the participation needed to protect her investors, it became clear that any expression of the Bank's intentions that had come out of her face-to-face meeting in New York had been illusory. Out of options and out of time, Alex emailed HanaTech's board:

> "We don't see how we can participate at a $2 million level. Our LPs will never support what you've done, nor will they ever understand how you've gone about it."

Alex wondered how she would inform her LPs (who had offered to provide the entire financing on better terms) that the Bank had taken 83 percent of the financing, while allocating to her LPs just 4 percent, when their stake in HanaTech was 40 percent of the Bank's. Suddenly, the CEO called to report that the Bank had decided to delay funding—and might not even fund after all, warning ominously:

> "They might not fund the business unless you assure them you won't sue. I've never asked you for a favor. All I've ever done is create value. Don't destroy it now. Don't damage everyone else. You have to tell them you won't sue over this transaction or you will blow up the company."

Alex faced a daunting dilemma. Through an orderly sale of HanaTech, she calculated that the AB Partner Fund stood to receive more than $50 million, suddenly reduced by the Bank's seemingly predatory preference on an apparently carefully orchestrated bridge loan. Running the numbers for Alex, the CEO appealed to Alex's larger interest: "Your Fund will only lose $3 million of value due to the Bank's unfair bridge. So it's still in your interest to give the Bank what they need."

Recalling Falstaff's famous line from *Henry IV*—"the better part of valor is discretion"—Alex sent off an email to the Bank. To settle down the CEO, she assured the Director that she would not sue the Bank. Then she followed up with a phone call. But the Director was not in. So she left a voicemail, confirming she would not sue. Within moments, she received an email from the Director's assistant:

"[The Director] will be out for the next two weeks and is totally unreachable."

Two members of the Bank's legal team called AB Partners' attorney, however, within minutes to say: "So, to be clear, AB Partners is *declining* to participate in the $4.7 million allocation that would have protected its LPs from dilution."

Alex's lawyer responded, "How could AB have declined what the Bank unilaterally withdrew?" With the lawyers' attempt to put words in Alex's mouth, the Director himself suddenly resurfaced from his heretofore "unreachable" two-week vacation, emailing Alex directly:

"I'm sorry you decided not to participate in the deal. As you know, HanaTech had to balance many factors from multiple constituencies, and that process determined the amount available for existing investors."

Curiously, the Director had used exactly the same phrasing his lawyers had just used. And his so-called "balancing of many factors" had resulted in wildly skewed economics in favor of the Bank, with significant harm to all other shareholders.

Soon HanaTech's CEO called Alex to advance a new threat on behalf of the Bank. Because its lawyers had determined that Alex's email and voicemail assurances were inadequate, the Bank had determined that it would withhold funding altogether. It informed the now-panicked CEO that it would not fund unless it received a "full release" from Alex and from AB Partners. *So much for "certainty of funding,"* Alex thought.

The Bank's lawyers followed up with an expansive release form that protected the Bank from any and all liability, no matter what. Alex had her attorneys send it back unsigned, informing the Bank that she would sign an edited version—if HanaTech's CEO reimbursed her LPs for profits lost if their participation were reduced from what the Bank had offered when she was in New York.

The CEO called Alex to complain that it wasn't fair that he'd have to personally cover her LPs for what he now termed "the Bank's theft." And of course, he was right. In Alex's opinion, the Bank had betrayed everyone—the CEO, HanaTech, the board, and the shareholders. But Alex's only duty was to her LPs.

As the deadline approached, who would blink? Unless Alex signed the Bank's expansive release, or the Bank withdrew its threat to seize the company, Sunday would be HanaTech's penultimate day in business. Alex was becoming increasingly confident that the Bank's threats were bully and bluster. Indeed, she even wondered if the value of a shareholder suit might exceed the value of AB Partners' stake in HanaTech.

But Alex also began to second-guess herself. Had she put her LPs' ownership interest at risk if the Bank followed through on its threat to liquidate the company? Should she have signed the release presented "at gunpoint"? Was there any way to get the board to reconsider her term sheet that provided protection to all shareholders? And if so, could she quickly reassemble AB Partners' financing? Or should she just take a $3 million "haircut" on her investment because of the Bank's clout and willingness to play hardball?

Alex hastily sent an email to HanaTech's CEO:

"The Bank is inappropriately leaning on you to pressure other shareholders. Please tell whoever at the Bank is having you do its bidding to call me directly from here on out. The problem at HanaTech is one of capital structure, in which the Bank has played the key role leading HanaTech into an artificial ditch. The fox is now in the henhouse preparing to feast on the chickens."

Frustrated with taking the blame for the Bank's betrayal of shareholders, Alex continued:

"Let me be absolutely clear on this: We have done everything in our power to protect all shareholders at every moment in this awful process. We have been fully prepared to fund not only an amount that would have protected our LPs from dilution, but also to fund a pro rata share of any rights offering made to all shareholders. So the narrative that AB Partners is holding things up had better stop immediately. And the record had better be corrected, before anyone does any more damage to our reputation."

· A WAY OUT OF THE TRAP ·

With her aggressive volley, Alex also offered the CEO a way out of the crisis by suggesting that the Bank:

1. Fund HanaTech as promised and correct the record with respect to any reputational damage to AB Partners.
2. Provide the math, methodology, and underlying principles the Bank followed in pricing and allocating the bridge loan financing to a leading litigation-support firm, where expert economists and financiers would quickly review and consent to

the validity of the transaction. This would provide
the Bank with a way free and clear of litigation—if,
in fact, its behavior had been fair, proper, and legal.

3. Provide shareholders with profits they would have
   received had they not been denied an opportunity
   to invest their pro rata share of the bridge-loan
   financing, which had been the Bank's proposed
   "intention."

· THE DENOUEMENT ·

Monday, the last day before the Bank's threatened foreclosure,
came and went . . . almost. Just before 9:00 p.m., Alex received
an email from the CEO:

> "I wanted to let you know that HanaTech is closing on
> the bridge financing tomorrow morning. The documents
> were revised over the weekend to allow HanaTech to sell
> up to $4.7 million of preferred shares to AB Partners on
> the same terms and conditions on which they were sold
> to other investors. The other investors in the financing
> were disappointed to learn that you were not initially
> offered your full pro rata share (as was their intention at
> the outset), and all parties have attempted to revise the
> financing to accommodate your investment. The Bank
> decreased its participation in this financing to make your
> participation possible."

Alex's relief was exceeded only by her shock at the revisionist email. She had protected her investors. However, the CEO's reframing of the Bank's conduct over the past week was stunning. The other investors had most certainly not been "disappointed to learn" that her investors had been taken advantage of, nor that the Bank's stated intent had been overlooked. And the "access to a full pro rata share" of the bridge loan had clearly not been made possible by the Bank's "decreased participation." Both were laughable claims. The Bank had reduced its participation by only $155,000. It was the other investors whose pro rata allocations had been reduced to allow AB Partner's LPs to take down its pro rata share of the bridge.

The bridge financing was funded the next day. Later that week, the Bank sent a formal notification to HanaTech's board reasserting its right to (re)install its junior associate on the board by returning the signed board approvals it had previously held back. Now the Bank was officially back on the board. And the crisis was over.

Having to spend a few days in the parallel universe of a Wall Street wolfpack nearly made Alex want to pitch her own tent in Zuccotti Park. The exercise of dealing with what Alex saw as the Bank's betrayal of shareholders required levels of legal advice and brinksmanship that were likely beyond the resources and experience of most businesspeople.

Alex reflected on what had unleashed a societal wave of anger at Wall Street and concluded that the human race had not necessarily come very far from Hobbes's description of most lives as solitary, poor, nasty, brutish, and short. As she recalled the "best and brightest" gazing into computer monitors in Manhattan skyscrapers, she thought they might well give world-class plunderers of past eras a run for their money.

· DISCUSSION QUESTIONS ·

1. Was the Bank, in fact, betraying shareholders, or was it merely being shrewd?
2. In an industry where the score is kept only by profit and loss, is there a role for ethics beyond what is imposed by law?
3. Was Alex a good steward when risking a lot ($50 million) for a little ($3 million)?
4. What other options might Alex have tried with the Bank, the CEO, and/or other shareholders?
5. Where did trust break down?
6. What could HanaTech, AB Partners, and Alex have done to guard against this betrayal?
7. What can they learn from this to better protect themselves in the future?

· · ·

CASE 2: A FIDUCIARY BREACH: MARIE JOHNSON VS. HER LAWYER

"Rather fail with honor than succeed by fraud."

—Sophocles

Before Bernie Madoff was found guilty of securities fraud and sentenced to one hundred and fifty years in prison for the largest Ponzi scheme in history, affinity fraud was a little-known term. Madoff preyed upon what the *New York Post* called "the Jewish circuit" of the well-heeled members of country clubs on Long Island and in Palm Beach. Drawing from an identifiable affinity group whose members tended to trust each other, Madoff took advantage of the trust bred by familiarity—be it derivative of religious affiliation, school ties, ethnicity, geography, or life circumstances.

Several years before Madoff was exposed, an Upper East Side couple who dodged Madoff's scam fell into a similar if less grandiose trap. After five years of relying on a young lawyer at a small Manhattan law firm, Sam and Marie Johnson (not their real names) hired Joe Cleveland (not his real name) to join them as full-time, in-house counsel. The Johnsons had come to know Joe on the board of a private school, where they, along with Joe, had a daughter attending. Sam and Marie attributed to their young lawyer all of the values of the school and the virtues of its philosophy about parenting and about life's priorities, especially where he spoke and wrote so convincingly about how he held those values, virtues, and priorities in the highest regard.

After Joe's five-year stint as the couple's personal lawyer, Sam and Marie were delighted to say yes when he asked for a job as their in-house counsel and fund manager. His frequent and solemn references to fiduciary duty—on top of years of faithful service as their personal attorney—made them comfortable in hiring the thirty-six-year-old. Their frequent mutual interactions with the neighborhood private school to which they all gave time and money added to their trust in Joe. Their plan was for Joe to set up an investment business the Johnsons would own, and from which Joe would receive a salary and performance incentives ("carried interests") above a preferred return to the couple for having put up all the money.

Alas, Joe was not the person they thought he was. And their misplaced trust in his character was partly their own fault, as they later learned when watching the Madoff affair unfold. In that sad case—as in their own—trustworthiness was attributed to someone by virtue of membership in a trusting affinity group.

· MARIE TRUSTS JOE LIKE FAMILY ·

In a note written soon after he was hired, Joe reassured the Johnsons that he *"always put the interests of the Johnson family ahead of his own."* So when he subsequently asked to be the only other signatory on Marie's personal bank account, she agreed. When he asked her for extensive power of attorney, she gave it. When he set himself up to be the sole manager of her separate assets, she was relieved, since her husband was preoccupied with out-of-state duties. Even when Joe wrote checks to himself out of Marie's personal bank account, she was unfazed. After all, she trusted him as her longtime legal counsel, as a friend, and as a representative to the parents' council of the private school their daughters attended.

Consistent with her unalloyed trust in Joe, Marie invited his wife to accompany her on an all-expenses-paid trip overseas. Marie loaned Joe $500,000 so he could coinvest in deals with her. With Joe's request for a bonus, Marie even forgave her half-million-dollar loan to him. (Unbeknownst to her, Joe then wrote a $1,000 check to himself from her bank account to pay himself for what he referred to as "legal work" in documenting her loan forgiveness. In a last-minute spasm of conscience, he voided the check, and Marie was none the wiser.) When Joe asked Marie to donate to a neighborhood charity and serve on its board, she agreed. And when she asked for legal advice on issues that arose with her duties at the school, he gave it.

· JOE BEGINS TO TEST THE WATERS ·

When an investment Joe made with the money Marie had loaned him began to falter, he quietly dumped it back into her account only months before writing it down by $12,500—all without a word to her. Thus, Joe came to realize that without any legal or financial training, Marie paid little attention to legal or financial matters. Indeed, she was busy raising a daughter, serving as president of an alumni group to which Joe belonged, and laboring in a humanitarian relief organization. And with Marie's husband frequently out of state, absorbed with his own projects and pursuing a significant nonbusiness career, Joe was free to manage Marie's assets however he saw fit. After all, that was his job—one of the main reasons Sam and Marie paid him. Before long—despite having brought no deals, no capital, and no track record to Johnson Capital—Joe began calling himself the founder of the couple's eponymous firm.

· JOE EXPANDS HIS ACTIVITIES TO SAM ·

After years of faithful service as a trusted fiduciary, Joe began to chafe. Learning that Sam would be in town for a few days, he drafted a transmittal memo to which he attached a legal document and a $300 personal check for his assistant to hand deliver to Sam. Within a sheaf of unrelated papers and documents for Sam's countersignature were the misleading transmittal memo, Joe's check, and a legal document referred to in Joe's memo. As usual, Joe attached a sticky note with his JC initials prominently displayed as "Reviewed and Approved," so Sam would know all legal documents were okay to sign.

This time, however, the system of blind trust was interrupted. As luck would have it, Sam had hired a new assistant who was unaware of the normal protocol by which Sam would sign whatever Joe placed in front of him with his initials on a "Reviewed and Approved" stamp. Rather than return the signed document directly to Joe's assistant, Sam's assistant ran it by Dave Parker, a recent hire at Johnson Capital. Dave quickly perceived that the legal document Sam had signed was different from the one Joe had identified in his transmittal instructions. Sensing that something was awry, Dave locked away the document for review with Sam when he returned.

In the meantime, Dave discovered that for his $300 check, Joe would have picked up a third of $2.5 million in cash on the Johnson Capital balance sheet. But that was only the tip of a large iceberg. Joe would also have ended up with a one-third ownership in the parent company to which the Johnsons had advanced millions of dollars when sponsoring third-party investment funds. Comparing the Johnsons' contribution with Joe's investment of $0, Dave couldn't understand why, for $300, Joe would, after more than a decade, suddenly own a one-third interest in the firm—much less why he'd acquire it by stealth.

When Dave alerted Sam that Joe was picking up a third of $2.5 million in exchange for a $300 personal check, Sam responded reflexively that Joe had to have made a mistake. Dave did a bit more sleuthing, however, and discovered that three years earlier, Joe had attempted to transfer to himself control of what he called a "worthless pass-through entity." At that time, when another employee had alerted Sam to Joe's undisclosed purchase, Sam had asked Joe how he could have thought it right to pick up an interest in any entity without talking with him about it first. Joe responded that it didn't really matter who owned the worthless entity, because "no economics flowed into it."

Sam had then instructed Joe never to assign ownerships—even worthless ones—without talking to him first. And suspecting nothing untoward, Sam had offered Joe an interest in the so-called worthless entity. But Joe had immediately transferred back to Sam all the ownership picked up clandestinely, as if it had been an inconsequential and innocent mistake. Thus Sam quickly forgot about the incident.

Sam now wondered if Joe's two attempts were related. Soon Dave confirmed that they both involved the same "worthless" entity. Joe had again attempted to transfer to himself an entity owned by Sam. This second time, rather than just assign the interests to himself without a word, Joe had written a false transmittal letter. Moreover, the entity in question was anything but "worthless." Not only did it possess millions in cash, but it was also the control entity for the fifteen-year-old firm the Johnsons had founded and funded from the beginning.

Now certain of Joe's betrayal, Sam confronted him, walked him to the elevator, and locked him out of his office. More from sadness than anger, Sam encouraged Joe to hire a good defense lawyer, offering him a fourteen-day standstill to allow him quietly to either settle up his accounts or prepare to defend himself in court. Joe quickly settled, and within a year was given an out-of-state assignment by an institution to which he and the Johnsons both belonged, making less awkward their occasional contact with other members of their common affinity group.

With Joe removed as longtime gatekeeper on all books, records, and electronic files, Dave was free to do an analysis of pending transactions. Soon he came across a written proposal Joe and his two lieutenants had put together, in which they'd made an offer to buy out the Small Business Administration's interests in investments in which Johnson Capital had been the sponsor. The offer was for $42,000. When Dave reported this value, Sam quizzed one of Joe's lieutenants, who responded, "We always 'sandbag' the numbers." Stunned, Sam researched the true value of the interests and soon contacted the SBA to offer more than $2.1 million for the Agency's interest—fifty times what Joe had presented as fair value.

This left Sam with little choice but to also terminate both of Joe's lieutenants who'd signed off on the manifestly phony value. This, too, was awkward, since they were both Upper East Side neighbors with multiple affinity connections. Not wanting to expose the embarrassing discovery within the affinity group, Sam presented them with the deal Joe had taken. Instead of agreeing to it, however, both contacted Joe, now out of state. And to Sam's surprise, both lieutenants filed specious preemptive lawsuits. One was quickly defeated in arbitration; but the other persisted, thanks to Joe's prescience—he had set up insurance to cover fiduciary breach claims. His lieutenant's cost-free attack would soon turn out to have great strategic value to Joe.

· MOVING $30 MILLION FROM THE JOHNSONS ·

The worst was yet to come. Marie soon discovered that Joe had hired David Smith, a partner in her estate-planning firm, to "represent" her in the transfer of her most valuable asset to Joe and his two lieutenants. Remarkably, Smith was a close friend of one of Joe's lieutenants whom he had long represented. Smith had never met—nor would ever meet—the Johnsons. When Marie finally sued Joe to recover the value of her transferred asset, Smith swore that he—not Joe—had "represented Mrs. Johnson" in what arbitrators would later rule had been an "unfair, interested-party transaction" that had represented a "breach of fiduciary duty."

Joe argued that Marie had had legitimate legal representation—however lousy—in the unfair transfer, so Joe was not liable for her remarkably unfair deal. Furthermore, Joe testified that though Marie thought Joe was her attorney, he wasn't including during all the years in which he'd transferred her assets to himself, sold failing assets back to her, and written checks to himself on her account.

In Joe's largest transfer to himself, he had moved Marie's most valuable asset over a weekend in her absence and prior to Sam's return from out of state. He'd documented the transfer by burying a false lowball value within a composite bookkeeping entry, camouflaged by four other assets transferred at current fair-market values (as required by law and in equity). By the time the Johnsons arrived five days after the transfer, Joe had already booked the interested-party transaction as a never-to-be-reviewed capital account credit.

Within the month, Joe and his lieutenants swore that the value of Marie's shares had ballooned in value from $0.6 million to $4.9 million. However, in discovery, Marie found a spreadsheet created by one of the insider director-transferees in which he'd calculated—*prior* to their transfer—an eight-times-higher $4.9 million value for Marie's shares.

In an impressive display of sophistry, both Joe and his lieutenant then swore under oath—unchallenged by Marie's lawyer—that on the day of transfer, her shares were *"absolutely"* no longer worth the higher value the board itself had formally established nineteen days prior to transfer.

A transactional lawyer by training, Joe Cleveland took great precautions to keep his fingerprints off the fraudulent Sunday transfer, as follows:

1. He resigned abruptly as a director a week after a co-insider board member (and his lieutenant) showed Marie's shares to be worth $4.9 million.

2. On the Friday *before* the Sunday transfer— suddenly no longer a Board member—Joe told Nate Smith, lawyer for the fund that owned

Marie's shares, that he would personally take over moving the fund's investments to another fund in which Joe's interests were higher (and where Nate was also fund counsel).

3. On transfer Sunday, Joe moved five assets (including Marie's vastly appreciated shares) into the new fund in which Joe and his lieutenants would instantaneously capture millions of dollars of concealed value.

4. On the Friday morning *after* the Sunday transfer, Joe retained David Smith from Marie's estate-planning law firm to pretend to represent her after he had just represented the largest transferee of her shares.

5. On the Friday afternoon after the Sunday transfer was complete, Joe caught the Johnsons en route to a wedding-anniversary celebration, asking the couple to drop by the office to sign a stack of documents, never letting on that:

    a. They were signing away millions in current value that he and his insider board-member lieutenants had hidden by using phony capital account credits.

    b. He had made the transfers himself and hired two conflicted affinity lawyers to pretend to represent (1) Marie and (2) the fund that owned her shares.

c. The conflicted affinity lawyers selected operated without engagement letters, conflict waivers, or any communication with their unwitting clients.

Less than two years later, the three insider directors (including Joe) pocketed over $30 million for having booked a $5 per share capital account credit for shares they now sold for $80 apiece.

Unsurprisingly, Joe moved to have Marie's case presented to arbitrators rather than to a jury. The judge overseeing arbitration had recently been an official in the same cozy affinity group where Joe was presently an officer. Consistent with the dense affinity network within which Joe operated, the judge did not recuse himself and, unsurprisingly, upheld the *only* defense arbitrators allowed—a technicality: The Johnsons had not caught Joe in time, given his fiduciary control over all books, records, electronic files, and the lieutenants who gave reports to the Johnsons.

· AFFINITY FRAUD ·

It seemed to Marie that cozy affinity connections had combined to betray her, playing a starring role in Joe's defense. Among the affinity-group members who either benefited from or helped to orchestrate, defend, and/or assist with what arbitrators ruled to have been an "unfair, interested-party transaction," were:

1. Marie's fund manager and longtime lawyer (Joe).
2. Both of Joe's lieutenants, who were insider directors of the company whose shares they transferred to themselves at a known false value.
3. Nate Smith, fund lawyer for both the transferor and the transferee fund.
4. David Smith, posing as Marie's counsel despite his roles as lawyer and close friend to the largest recipient of Marie's massively undervalued shares.
5. Joe's defense counsel, another affinity connection (belonging to the same affinity group as the conflicted lawyers and the supervising judge).
6. Joe's "expert witness," a high-ranking affinity-group member who provided a veneer of affinity approval (along with giving Joe a 60 percent discount on his fees).
7. The judge overseeing arbitration, who'd recently held the same official position in their common affinity group as Joe now held.

Joe's defense attorney (likewise a high-ranking affinity-group member) made a posttrial appeal to the arbitration firm to dump the panel chairman, whose questions made clear that he was troubled not only by Joe's manifest breach of fiduciary duty, but also by his destruction of evidence when contacted by counsel. Furthermore, the panel chairman was not part of Joe's affinity network. He was dumped from the panel after trial because Joe's defense attorney complained that he sat on a parent school board with one of Marie's sons-in-law. Somehow this served as justification enough for the arbitration firm (represented by another member of Joe's affinity group) to accede to the appeal to dismiss the panel chairman before he could participate in the panel's ruling.

Immediately prior to arbitration, the judge in whose court Joe's lieutenant's preemptive filing had been assigned, also came to Joe's rescue, ruling that the Johnsons' counterclaims (though later proven valid) were time-barred. Thus, mere days prior to Joe's arbitration, this judge issued a summary judgment dismissing the Johnsons' damages by virtue of the statute of limitations—even though time limits are normally tolled when dealing with fiduciaries.

What arbitrators ruled had been Joe's "only accepted defense" was a technicality that allowed him to keep the money he had taken when giving Marie a $0.6 million bookkeeping credit for shares he and his lieutenants swore twenty-nine days later—under penalty of perjury—had a fair-market value (FMV) of $4.9 million.

Delighted with all the help from his affinity network, Joe broadcast to affinity-group members that the verdict had been a "miracle of significant proportions," identifying "intercession" as the reason he'd kept his share of a $30+ million interested-party transaction. Adding insult to injury, Joe trashed Marie to another affinity-group official as a "vengeful and vindictive woman" whose "claims could not be sustained." As soon as Joe returned from his out-of-state assignment, his lieutenant settled the suit he'd filed that had secured for Joe his "only accepted defense."

Marie discovered that the affinity group to which belonged (1) the beneficiaries of Marie's misfortune, (2) the lawyers who covered for them, and (3) the relevant judges, defense attorneys, and experts enjoyed a well-earned reputation for affinity fraud; she joined other trusting victims of those defrauded by members of the same group.

To put the affinity nightmare behind the Johnsons, Sam sent forgiveness letters to all who'd benefited from the adjudicated breach.

· DISCUSSION QUESTIONS ·

1. Should the Johnsons have pursued an appeal rather than send out forgiveness letters to those who had benefited from an adjudicated breach of fiduciary duty? Why or why not?

2. Should Marie have hired a lawyer to respond to Joe's report to group officials that she was "a vengeful and vindictive woman"?

3. Did the cozy affinity relationships between (1) Joe, (2) his lieutenants, and (3) the conflicted lawyers he retained make betrayal more or less likely? more or less easy to overcome?

4. If you were Marie and learned that shares your fund manager and lawyer sold for $80 apiece were ones he'd transferred from you on a Sunday in your absence by giving you a bookkeeping credit of $5 apiece, what would you have done?

5. Since Joe had made the unfair transfer on a Sunday with the help of conflicted affinity lawyers pretending to represent you, would you seek to recover damages from the law firms who also betrayed your interests?

CONCLUSION

Robert Louis Stevenson once observed, "Compromise is the best and cheapest lawyer." This is wise counsel to entrepreneurial leaders who hope to build their careers on high-trust relationships, yet end up in conflict or betrayal.

Having observed two litigators up close, I've been struck by the differences between the two regarding their competence, spirit, and quality. In the first instance, I came away with a high regard for litigators as honorable advocates. Though litigation was still a miserable experience, I could see that my attorney was smart, tough, honest, and determined. He gave a brilliant opening statement that nearly won the case on its own. His depositions were thorough, and his cross-examinations were devastating and done without regard to station. Moreover, he carefully disclosed conflicts and prior relationships. As a result, the judge and opposing counsel respected him. And by the end of the prosecution's presentation of its case-in-chief, the judge called everyone into chambers to urge settlement—even before my attorney had begun to present my case.

In the second instance, the lawyer barely gave an opening statement. What he said was perfunctory, incomplete, and forgettable. He protected a former client by allowing him to carve out vital evidence and give unchallenged testimony. As might be expected, opposing counsel and judges showed little respect for him, resulting in virtually every pretrial motion going against him. Predictably, he declined to appeal anything.

Both attorneys set up a mock trial to dry run the persuasiveness of their arguments and the strength of their evidence. In the case of my lawyer, his presentation was crisp, persuasive, and winning. In the case of the second lawyer, he was so disorganized that when an advisor to the plaintiff stepped in to present the vital information he had omitted, the mock judges reversed their ruling, deeming the defendant's actions not merely unethical but, in fact, criminal.

I summarize these wildly disparate litigation experiences so that entrepreneurial leaders may be aware of the wide range of competence and ethical behavior at work in the justice system. If entrepreneurs must hire litigation counsel, they should go with only the best. As Robert Frost noted, "A jury consists of twelve persons chosen to decide who has the better lawyer."

If you cannot settle a betrayal outside of litigation, the recommended course of action—for both economic and emotional reasons—is to find a smart, honest lawyer who is respected by the judiciary. Then buckle up for a long and miserable chapter of your life.

· ACKNOWLEDGMENTS ·

I F THERE ARE USEFUL takeaways in this short book, they have their origins in my upbringing. My parents trusted me long before I deserved their trust. They made it hard to let them down. I now see they knew what they were doing when teaching me to love the feeling of being trustworthy—as much as I hated letting them down.

Before long, parents of my friends allowed their kids to go places if I went along. That's because, in the words of these parents, my presence was akin to "having a forty-year-old chaperone along." While I hated this brand at the time, I now look back on it as a reflection of a mindset that has served me well throughout my adult life.

I've raised seven kids, believing in them before they might have been worthy of my trust. I was certain of their eventual trustworthiness, and even when they disappointed, I was confident of their ability to "figure it out," given enough time and support. Rarely have they disappointed me for long—and their love and worldviews have made me a better person.

In business, over the course of nearly fifty years, I've had more than three hundred partners all over the world. Only a tiny handful have proven untrustworthy. Dealing with employees, suppliers, distributors, lenders, bankers, lawyers, doctors, and other teammates has been gratifying—even if not perfect. In most cases, trust builds trustworthiness, which further enhances trust and makes doing business more profitable, more efficient, and more pleasant. I'm grateful to all who have helped me strengthen a feedback loop I've always believed was the best way to do business and to live life.

I also want to thank the thousands of students I've taught over the past twenty-three years at the Stanford Graduate School of Business. They're uniformly bright, idealistic, capable, and worthy of our hope, optimism—and trust. The world is in good hands with this next generation, which has taught me to believe we're in better hands than some headlines might suggest.

While I've lived a life in which the fruits of trust have been abundant, I've also experienced betrayal, which has taught me a lot about trust too—whom to trust, how far to trust, and how to repair strained trust. I'm thankful for (not *to*) the scoundrels I've known and for having survived their worst and refined my approach to trust.

Many friends and colleagues were willing to read over my various drafts and musings. I appreciate all of it—and the book is better for it. Bob Whitman—my partner for three decades at Trammell Crow, on the board at FranklinCovey, and as a cofounder of Whitman Peterson—has been a paragon of trust and trustworthiness. Stephen Covey wrote the foreword to this book, and it's an honor for me to have it; he has contributed to the power and speed of trust for a generation.

Charles O'Reilly, my colleague at Stanford with whom I've cotaught a leadership course for the past decade, has continually sharpened my thinking. And Rod Kramer, another Stanford colleague, who had already plowed the ground on the dynamics of organizational trust, was a superb reviewer of an early draft, taking time to provide both academic studies and real-life examples that bolstered this book. I'm grateful as well to Jeff Pfeffer at Stanford, with whom I disagree on many leadership topics but whose provocative approach I admire, without which I might never have written out my experiences with trust.

Peter Robinson, a Senior Fellow at the Hoover Institution, along with his business partner Joe Malchow, were willing to weigh in early on to encourage me to put words to paper and to refine them. Jim Hnat, our former general counsel at JetBlue, was an early editor who forced me to hone my imprecise thinking. The comments of my lifelong friend, Randy Paul, proved invaluable.

I'm grateful to Stephen S. Power at AMACOM, who had the idea in the first place and reached out to me to write a book on my approach to building high-trust enterprises. Were it not for him, this book would not exist.

Most of all, I must thank my wife Diana—the best partner one could have. She's seen me through ups and downs, and has trusted me to find my bearings each time I lose them. She was a key partner in writing this book—both getting my ideas on paper and refining how to say them. Along those lines, I am grateful to David A. Kaplan, whose ability to write clearly, to find examples, and to push back on fuzzy thinking has been invaluable. His good humor and energy have never failed as we partnered to produce this book.

For this second edition, I thank Stanford case writer Jeff Conn, who helped with the two cases, and Scott Miller of FranklinCovey who worked with Adam Merrill and team to develop the organizational-trust diagnostic. Alex Peterson, my daughter-in-law, kept everything on track, and HarperCollins—who bought AMACOM and, thus, the first edition of *The 10 Laws of Trust*—was a pleasure to work with when publishing this second edition.

Finally, to all the many partners, colleagues, friends, and business associates who have unfailingly gone the extra mile as fiduciaries, service providers, and companion travelers, I owe a huge debt. As I've occasionally navigated bumpy and uncertain roads, I've been impressed that most people do their utmost to be worthy of our trust when granted it. I'm grateful to have concluded that living a life of high-trust relationships is a goal that's achievable. And overcoming the occasional betrayal of trust is possible. That is the central message of this book.

· ENDNOTES ·

THE POWER OF TRUST

1. David Sloan Wilson and Edward O. Wilson, "Rethinking the Theoretical Foundation of Sociobiology," *The Quarterly Review of Biology* 82, no. 4 (2007): 327–48.
2. Jeffrey Pfeffer, *Power: Why Some People Have It—and Others Don't* (New York: Harper Business, 2010).

LAW 2
INVEST IN RESPECT

1. Alex Pentland, *Social Physics: How Good Ideas Spread—The Lessons from a New Science* (New York: Penguin Books, 2014).

LAW 3
EMPOWER OTHERS

1. Amy Edmonson, "Strategies for Learning from Failure," *Harvard Business Review*, April 2011, https://hbr.org/2011/04/strategies-for-learning-from-failure.

2. Fernando Flores and Robert C. Solomon, "Creating Trust," *Business Ethics Quarterly* 8, no. 2 (January 23, 2015): 205.

3. Carol Dweck, *Mindset: The New Psychology of Success* (New York: Ballantine Books, 2007).

LAW 5

CREATE A COMMON DREAM

1. Scott T. Allison and George R. Goethals, *Heroes: What They Do and Why We Need Them* (New York: Oxford University Press, 2011).

2. Peter S. Beagle, *The Last Unicorn* (New York: Roc, Penguin Books, 1991).

3. Howard Schultz and Joanne Gordon, *Onward: How Starbucks Fought for Its Life Without Losing Its Soul* (New York: Rodale Books, 2011).

LAW 6

KEEP EVERYONE INFORMED

1. Don Tapscott and Anthony D. Williams, *Radical Openness: Four Unexpected Principles for Success* (New York: TED Conferences, 2013).

2. Jim Daily, "Why Radical Openness Is Unnerving and Necessary: A Q&A with TED eBook Authors Don Tapscott and Anthony D. Williams," *TED Blog*, January 24, 2013, https://blog.ted.com/why-radical-openness-is-unnerving-reshaping-and -necessary-a-qa-with-ted-ebook-authors-don-tapscott-and -anthony-d-williams/.

LAW 7

EMBRACE RESPECTFUL CONFLICT

1. Jerry Hirshberg, *The Creative Priority: Putting Innovation to Work in Your Business* (London: Penguin Books, 1999).

LAW 9

STRIVE FOR WIN-WIN NEGOTIATIONS

1. Roger Fisher and William Ury, *Getting to Yes: Negotiating Agreement Without Giving In* (New York: Houghton Mifflin, 1981).

LAW 10

FIX BREACHES IMMEDIATELY

1. Max De Pree, *Leading Without Power: Finding Hope in Serving Community* (San Francisco: Jossey-Bass, 2003).

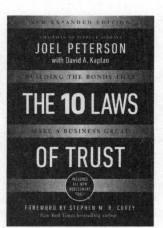